IMAGES
of America

CAMP DAVID

Camp David encompasses an area of approximately 180 acres and includes guest cabins, recreational facilities, barracks, a helipad, and operations buildings. (Google Maps.)

ON THE COVER: Aspen Lodge is the president's residence at Camp David. Originally a conglomeration of rustic structures named "The Bear's Den" by Pres. Franklin D. Roosevelt, Aspen has evolved into a modern, comfortable abode. In this photograph, Pres. Lyndon Johnson is standing on Aspen's patio with guests during a visit to Camp David by Australian prime minister Harold Holt and his wife. (Courtesy of Lyndon B. Johnson Presidential Library.)

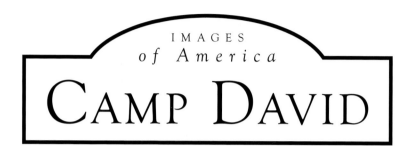

IMAGES
of America

CAMP DAVID

Robert P. Savitt

ARCADIA
PUBLISHING

Copyright © 2024 by Robert P. Savitt
ISBN 978-1-4671-6087-2

Published by Arcadia Publishing
Charleston, South Carolina

Printed in the United States of America

Library of Congress Control Number: 2023944204

For all general information, please contact Arcadia Publishing:
Telephone 843-853-2070
Fax 843-853-0044
E-mail sales@arcadiapublishing.com

Visit us on the Internet at www.arcadiapublishing.com

For Todd: my big brother, my best friend.

Contents

ACKNOWLEDGMENTS

I am grateful to the very knowledgeable and helpful personnel at several presidential libraries and other National Archives facilities. These include Zachary Roberts (George H.W. Bush), Mary Finch (George H.W. Bush), Sarah Barca (George W. Bush), Tally Fugate (George W. Bush), Victoria Cacchione (Jimmy Carter), Keith Shuler (Jimmy Carter), Brittany Parris (Jimmy Carter), Sara Mitchell (Jimmy Carter), Herbert Ragan (Bill Clinton), Michelle Kopfer (Dwight Eisenhower), James Ginther (Dwight Eisenhower), Mary Burtzloff (Dwight Eisenhower), Elizabeth Druga (Gerald Ford), Stacy Davis (Gerald Ford), Allen Fisher (Lyndon Johnson), Jenna DeGraffenried (Lyndon Johnson), Sarah Cunningham (Lyndon Johnson), Stacey Chandler (John F. Kennedy), Billy Wade (National Archives, College Park), Ryan Pettigrew (Richard Nixon), Elizabeth Macias (Richard Nixon), Lindsey Donaldson (National Park Service, Catoctin Mountain Park), Katie Wackrow (National Park Service, Catoctin Mountain Park), Matthew Hanson (Franklin D. Roosevelt), and Laurie Austin (Harry Truman).

I would also like to thank the many people who have graciously provided photographs and insights, including John Kinnaird, Vicky Grinder, Doug Propheter, Elizabeth Comer, and Amy Whitney. In addition, I have often consulted a very fine internet blog called *About Camp David*.

Several excellent books have provided valuable information and insights into the history and operation of Camp David, including Michael Giorgione's *Inside Camp David* and W. Dale Nelson's *The President Is at Camp David*. I have also utilized many of the fine publications of the National Park Service regarding the history and operation of sites relevant to Camp David and its surroundings.

INTRODUCTION

On July 5, 1942, at a location in the mountains near Thurmont, Maryland, President Roosevelt signed a document entitled "U.S.S. Shangri La—Launched at Catoctin, July 5, 1942." This "vessel" was not designed to sail the seven seas; rather, it was intended to serve as a place for US presidents to escape temporarily from the nation's pressure-cooker capital—Washington, DC.

Thurmont, of course, is not a seaport, and the vessel is not a seafaring ship. The "USS Shangri La" is a mountaintop hideaway created during World War II as a substitute for the vulnerable presidential yacht. FDR, a former assistant secretary of the Navy, authorized the conversion of a former campground to a presidential retreat run by Navy personnel. Through its many alterations in its over 80 years of service, Shangri La has continued as a Navy site, officially designated Naval Support Facility, Thurmont Maryland. The name Shangri La was changed to Camp David in 1953 by Pres. Dwight D. Eisenhower in honor of his father and grandson. It has served each president since FDR and has been the scene of several historic meetings, including most notably the negotiation in 1978 of a peace treaty between Egypt and Israel known as the Camp David Accords.

Some presidents have loved the mountain retreat and others not so much. Pres. Ronald Reagan used it more than any other president—571 days during his eight years in office. Presidents Bush 41 and 43 held many happy family gatherings (and even a wedding!) at the camp. Pres. Harry Truman found it to be dark and confining, largely because of the thick growth around the main lodge. He felt more comfortable after some thinning and opening up of the terrain, but was never enthusiastically drawn to it.

Over the years, many improvements have been made to the original, rustic facilities, and new buildings have been erected to meet developing needs. FDR's bedroom was originally fitted with a hinged wall to serve as an emergency door large enough to accommodate his wheelchair in case of fire. President Eisenhower—an avid golfer—added a three-hole course to the compound. The old swimming pool was replaced with a heated pool during Pres. Richard Nixon's administration. President Reagan converted some of the retreat's paths into horseback riding trails.

The ability to communicate with Washington is, of course, a vital necessity when the president is at the camp. Roosevelt had a telephone in his bedroom for outgoing calls to Washington. Incoming calls were received by the camp's switchboard personnel who, if necessary, would notify the president. FDR then would use his bedroom phone to connect with the caller. This archaic system has been upgraded through the years and now ensures that the president can quickly and effectively communicate with anyone, anywhere.

Presidents have met their religious needs by traveling to a church in nearby Thurmont or worshipping in a makeshift chapel at Hickory Lodge, one of the camp's original buildings. In 1991, using privately raised funds, a beautiful nondenominational facility—Evergreen Chapel— was opened on-site.

One of the reasons the Catoctin Mountains were chosen as the site for the presidential retreat was the proximity to Washington. When Shangri La opened in 1942, FDR traveled to the camp by automobile. The final stretch of the two-hour trip was over dirt roads. President Truman sometimes enjoyed driving himself, closely followed by Secret Service vehicles. President Eisenhower initiated the use of helicopters to reach Camp David, reducing the travel time to about 30 minutes.

The peaceful atmosphere and abundance of facilities provide presidents with a place where they and their families can experience "normal" life away from the public eye. FDR worked on his stamp collection, Eisenhower fished and golfed, Nixon bowled, George H.W. Bush pitched horseshoes, George W. Bush went mountain biking, Ronald Reagan rode horses, and the Ford family engaged in virtually all the recreational opportunities available at the camp. Jimmy Carter sledded with his daughter, Bill Clinton practiced his golf swing, and Barack Obama played basketball.

With its remote location away from the turbulence of presidential life in Washington, Camp David also served as a place for quiet contemplation and uninterrupted meetings with staff members. Many State of the Union addresses and other important speeches were prepared at the camp.

The retreat has also become a popular venue for visits by foreign leaders and a site for important international meetings. Jimmy Carter and Bill Clinton hosted meetings with Israeli and Arab heads of state. Barack Obama hosted the G8 Summit at Camp David in 2012. Mikhail Gorbachev visited Reagan, and Vladimir Putin met with George W. Bush at Camp David.

For US Navy personnel, a tour of duty at Camp David provides a once-in-a-lifetime experience. A notice in a US Seabee publication described the presidential retreat as a "Historically Unique Duty Station" and noted that service at Camp David offers "an opportunity to join a team of dedicated, hand-picked Navy professionals" who provide "world-class service to the President."

US presidents are never off duty. Wherever and whenever they go, the responsibilities of the office travel with them. As head of state and commander in chief of the armed forces, the president must be prepared to act and react at all times. Presidents are continuously scrutinized and are rarely out of the public eye.

Ronald Reagan once likened a president's life in Washington to being a bird in a gilded cage. "That's why," he said, "so many presidents . . . on weekends go to Camp David, where you can get back to a normal house and open a front door and walk out in the yard if you want to, take a hike and do things of that kind."

It is easy to understand why our nation's leaders enjoy going for a sail on the USS Shangri La.

One

IN THE BEGINNING

BEFORE SHANGRI LA

The winter of 1935 was marked by heavy snowfall in Frederick County, Maryland. By February, 12 inches of snow lay on the ground, making travel and commerce extremely difficult. Nevertheless, a group of intrepid federal government officers made their way into Frederick City to begin a process that ultimately resulted in the establishment of a US national park, a Maryland state park, and a retreat for US presidents.

The group was tasked with acquiring a large tract of rugged land in the nearby Catoctin Mountains. The land had been used primarily for farming and as a source of timber for many years. Overuse and poor practices, along with natural disasters such as the chestnut tree blight, made the land barely usable for farming and virtually unusable as a source of timber. As part of President Roosevelt's New Deal, a plan was developed to purchase the land and create a recreational facility for use by a variety of people and organizations.

The project manager, Mike Williams, moved into a residence on Church Street in Frederick and began developing a property acquisition plan. A team of acquisition officers soon arrived and set out to find and appraise tracts of land in the nearby Catoctin Mountains. When sites were identified and appraised, the government agents made purchase offers to local farmers and landowners.

While many were willing to part with their property, others resisted. In some cases, residents were reluctant to move from land that had long been in their families. Others resented what they deemed as government pressure to take over their land. Local government officials feared that government ownership would significantly reduce tax revenues. Finally, in addition to these local issues, bureaucratic entanglements and rivalries within the federal government slowed the project.

Ultimately, the acquisition team was able to convince many landowners that the benefits of selling land that was marginally productive outweighed most objections. Local officials were persuaded that the loss of tax revenue would be more than offset by the lowered cost of maintaining services and providing relief to owners of under-producing land. Furthermore, the construction and operation of facilities within the new recreational demonstration area would provide many jobs for local residents.

The Catoctin Recreational Demonstration Area that emerged from these actions consisted of three camp areas: Misty Mount, Greentop, and Hi-Catoctin. Each met the original purpose of this New Deal project by providing a welcome retreat for groups ranging from disabled children to city-bound federal employees. The uses dramatically changed with the onset of World War II. Two of the camps—Misty Mount and Greentop—served military-related functions. The third—Hi-Catoctin—became the subject of this book.

In 1776, Thomas Johnson—the future first governor of Maryland—and his three brothers established the Catoctin Iron Furnace near what is today the community of Thurmont, Maryland. During the furnace's 127 years of operation, it produced iron for the cannons and cannonballs used by George Washington's Revolutionary War army, machinery for the first vessel to utilize steam power, plates used on the Union ironclad ship *Monitor* during the Civil War, and the material used in the production of Franklin stoves. During its first century, the furnace was fueled by charcoal from trees logged in the surrounding Catoctin Mountains. In 1873, coal became the furnace's source of fuel. In the 30 years before its closing, the furnace produced iron for the manufacture of items such as car wheels. However, the many years of heavy timber cutting, along with forest fires, the destructive chestnut tree blight, and poor land management rendered the land around it submarginal for logging and farming. The Catoctin Iron Furnace closed in 1903. (Courtesy of Catoctin Furnace Historical Society.)

Prohibition in the United States led to the establishment of a furtive whiskey industry in the Catoctin Mountains. In the summer of 1929, an incident involving liquor, a romantic entanglement, a raid gone bad, and the death of a local law enforcement officer captured headlines around the country. (Author's collection.)

With its refreshing summertime temperatures, the Catoctin Mountains attracted an increasing number of vacationers during the 1920s and 1930s. A number of local residents took advantage of this by turning their homes into vacation establishments offering room, board, and recreational activities. In a widely sensationalized incident that attracted nationwide attention in 1933, a cottage owner named Bessie Darling was mysteriously shot and killed in her establishment. (Author's collection.)

In 1929, Wilbur Freeze established one of the earliest motels in the area to take advantage of the burgeoning automobile tourism trade. His Cozy Inn in Thurmont began as Camp Cozy with three cabins and soon grew to 15. With the establishment of the nearby presidential retreat, the Cozy became a popular base for media personnel during periods when the president was in residence. (Author's collection.)

The little town of Thurmont had long been a traditional rural population center serving the surrounding Catoctin Mountain community. In the post–World War I period, as automobile travel grew in popularity, the town increasingly became a launch point for the growing number of travelers to the Catoctin region. This photograph shows Main Street as it appeared in the 1930s. (Courtesy of Thurmont Images.)

In a number of areas around the country, large tracts of land were reduced to marginal usefulness due to overuse of soil and intensive timber cutting. The Roosevelt administration developed a plan to convert 39 of these sites into parks, camps, and other leisure-activity facilities. In 1935, as part of this program, government agents purchased tracts of land in the mountains near Frederick and created Catoctin Recreational Demonstration Area (Catoctin RDA). (Courtesy of National Park Service, Catoctin Mountain Park.)

Many of the properties purchased by the federal government were "home places" that had been owned by families for many generations. Tract No. 9 (pictured) was one of the parcels incorporated into the Catoctin RDA. (Courtesy of National Park Service, Catoctin Mountain Park.)

Two New Deal agencies were charged with building and developing the facilities at the Catoctin RDA. Between 1936 and 1938, laborers provided by the Works Progress Administration (WPA) created the basic structures for Camps Misty Mount, Greentop, and Hi-Catoctin. Beginning in 1938, Civilian Conservation Corps (CCC) recruits further developed the RDA through activities such as cutting trails, reforesting, and assisting in a variety of maintenance and construction projects. The programs of the WPA and CCC served a dual purpose: reducing unemployment while engaging in worthy improvement projects. These images are from CCC files. (Both, courtesy of National Park Service, Catoctin Mountain Park.)

During the summers of 1939, 1940, and 1941, Camp Hi-Catoctin served as a vacation retreat for federal employees and their families (right). The facility had 18 rustic cabins that could accommodate 72 people. A one-week stay cost $14 for adults and $7 for children. Campers could rent bedding for 5¢ per item. Among the activities available were swimming, hiking, archery, badminton, Ping-Pong, croquet, and horseshoes. In a letter written 60 years after a family vacation at Hi-Catoctin, a woman fondly recalled her visit as an eight-year-old girl: The cabins were "pretty rustic with no electricity in individual cabins." Campers used "kerosene lanterns and flashlights to make our way to the wash rooms at night." "Hiking was a great sport then" and one of the many hiking destinations was the lodge where Bessie Darling was shot. The dining hall at Hi-Catoctin (below) was one of the few buildings with electricity. (Both, courtesy of National Park Service, Catoctin Mountain Park.)

VACATION AT.....
HI-CATOCTIN CAMP

THE CAMP ....

• PROVIDES A DELIGHTFUL AND INEXPENSIVE VACATION FOR FEDERAL EMPLOYEES AND THEIR FAMILIES IN THE COOL CATOCTIN MOUNTAINS.
• OFFERS A WEALTH OF RECREATIONAL ACTIVITY — SWIMMING, HIKING, NATURE-LORE, CAMPFIRES, SOFTBALL, ARCHERY, BADMINTON, DRAMATICS, MUSIC, FOLK-DANCING, ETC.
• IS IN PICTURESQUE FOREST LAND WITH MOUNTAIN TRAILS, REFRESHING STREAMS AND RUSTIC CABINS.
• SEASON BEGINS JULY 7, 1940.
• SPECIAL CAMP PERIOD FOR CHILDREN (8 TO 14 YEARS) — JUNE 24 - JULY 3.

— oOo —

DIRECTED BY THE FEDERAL CAMP COUNCIL
OPERATED BY THE WELFARE AND RECREATIONAL ASSOCIATION
FOR APPLICATION CARD OR ADDITIONAL INFORMATION — CALL NATIONAL 7363
....
TEAR OFF AND ADDRESS TO HI-CATOCTIN CAMP OFFICE
1135 - 21ST STREET, N.W.

NAME . . . .

ADDRESS. . . . .

A key factor in the choice of Camp Hi-Catoctin for the presidential retreat was the existence of facilities that could be reused in the new compound, significantly reducing the cost of construction. Among the reusable structures were guest cabins that had been built as part of the Hi-Catoctin camp for federal employees. (Courtesy of National Park Service, Catoctin Mountain Park.)

During summer months, the Maryland League for Crippled Children leased Camp Greentop and used it as a summer retreat for disabled youngsters. Swimming in the modern pool provided both fun and physical therapy and was one of the most popular activities for campers. (Courtesy of National Park Service, Catoctin Mountain Park.)

Two

SHANGRI LA

FDR AND HARRY S. TRUMAN

On the afternoon of April 22, 1942, a little over four months after the Japanese attack on Pearl Harbor, a five-car convoy snaked its way up a mountainside in rural Maryland. At the top of the mountain, the vehicles stopped, and the occupants emerged. Several hours later, the cars descended and drove toward the nation's capital.

Three weeks later, the mountaintop was abuzz with activity. As was later learned, Franklin D. Roosevelt, the president of the United States, had been a passenger in one of the cars. In his first nine years in office, he was able occasionally to escape the climate and chaos of Washington, DC, for brief periods of quiet respite. During trips to his family home in Hyde Park, New York, and Warm Springs, Georgia, and on daylong cruises on the presidential yacht, FDR relaxed with friends, worked on his stamp collection, and carried out his responsibilities in the relative quiet of familiar surroundings. The outbreak of war severely altered these options. Trips to Hyde Park and Warm Springs took him far from the capital and use of the presidential yacht was deemed dangerous in light of the threat posed by German submarines.

As a substitute, the president and his advisors sought a relatively inexpensive site within an hour or two of Washington at an altitude high enough to provide relief from the heat and humidity of the nation's capital. The search was whittled down to three possibilities: one near Virginia's Shenandoah Mountains and two at Maryland's Catoctin Recreational Demonstration Area, near the small town of Thurmont. Camp Hi-Catoctin, at the recreational demonstration area, was by far the least expensive option since it already had cabins and other facilities on-site. With its 1,800-foot altitude, it was 5-10 degrees cooler than Washington. The location was approximately two hours from the White House by automobile, and its remoteness and thick forest surroundings offered a high degree of security. Roosevelt called the retreat Shangri La after the mystical paradise described in James Hilton's popular novel and movie *Lost Horizon*.

The president visited Shangri La a total of 64 days during his administration, and in addition to relaxing with friends and enjoying his hobbies, he hosted visits by several heads of state. His successor, Harry S. Truman, was not enamored with the retreat and traveled to Shangri La only 10 times during his nearly eight years in office. When vacationing at his "Little White House" in Key West, Florida, and his home in Independence, Missouri, Truman made Shangri La available to staff. The retreat was used nearly every week during his administration.

Throughout US history, presidents have found refuge from the political chaos of Washington, DC, in retreats ranging from their personal homes to vacation spots around the country. There they could relax with hobbies, recreation, or quiet reading and contemplation. During the first nine years of his presidency, FDR was able to escape the nation's capital through day trips on the presidential yacht, or for longer periods at either his family home in Hyde Park or a health spa in Warm Springs. Wartime considerations made it dangerous to cruise on the yacht and impractical to venture far from the Washington command center. A search for a secure, healthful location led to the establishment of the Shangri La presidential retreat in the Catoctin Mountains of Maryland. Pictured are the presidential yacht *Potomac* (above) and the Roosevelt family's Hyde Park estate (below). (Above, courtesy of Franklin D. Roosevelt Library; below, author's collection.)

FDR was an active participant in planning the main lodge at Shangri La. The existing building (17.5 feet by 28 feet) became a combined living and dining room. A bedroom wing, kitchen, and porch were constructed at angles extending from the living-dining room area. FDR asked that the beams be exposed in the dining area and porch. His sketch of the bedroom area (right) envisioned master and guest quarters with a bathroom in between. The bedroom was to have an emergency hinged exit so that the president could be moved outside quickly in the event of fire. In accordance with FDR's wishes, the camp was to be rustic and should utilize as much of the existing structures as possible. The main lodge and other buildings at Shangri La were furnished with simple items gathered largely from the naval storage facility in Washington, the presidential yacht, and the White House attic. The original budget estimate (below) reflects these cost-saving features. FDR annotated the estimate with check marks of approval, agencies to be involved, and directions on sleeping quarters. (Both, courtesy of Franklin D. Roosevelt Library.)

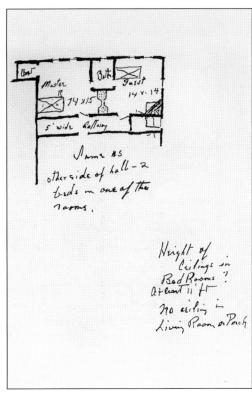

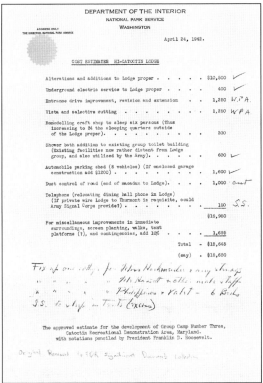

DEPARTMENT OF THE INTERIOR
NATIONAL PARK SERVICE
WASHINGTON

April 24, 1942.

COST ESTIMATES HI-CATOCTIN LODGE

Alterations and additions to Lodge proper	$10,500	✓
Underground electric service to Lodge proper	400	✓
Entrance drive improvement, revision and extension	1,250	W.P.A.
Vista and selective cutting	1,250	W P A
Remodelling craft shop to sleep six persons (Thus increasing to 34 the sleeping quarters outside of the Lodge proper).	200	
Shower bath addition to existing group toilet building (Existing facilities now rather distant from group, and also utilized by the Army).	600	✓
Automobile parking shed (8 vehicles) (If enclosed garage construction add $1200)	1,600	✓
Dust control of road (end of macadam to Lodge).	1,000	Out
Telephone (relocating dining hall phone in Lodge) (If private wire Lodge to Thurmont is requisite, could Army Signal Corps provide?)	160	S.S.
	$16,950	
For miscellaneous improvements in immediate surroundings, screen planting, walks, tent platforms (?), and contingencies, add 10%	1,695	
Total	$18,645	
(say)	$18,650	

Fix up one cottg. for Miss Hackmeister + any stnogs.
  "   "   "   "   Miss Hassett + other male stags
  "   "   "   "   Philippinos + Valet - 6 Beds
S.S. to sleep in Tents (exclus.)

The approved estimate for the development of Group Camp Number Three, Catoctin Recreational Demonstration Area, Maryland. with notations penciled by President Franklin D. Roosevelt.

Original Removed to FDR Signature Document collection

19

On April 30, 1942, eight days after his first visit to the future Shangri La, Roosevelt returned for an inspection visit. After reviewing construction plans, he gave his final approval to the project. The existing structures were easily movable, facilitating quick construction of the main lodge and preparation of several of the other cabins on the site. The camp structures were designed to accommodate about 40 people. In addition to the bedroom plan sketched by the president, there would be a 15-foot-by-18-foot screened porch situated to provide a view of the Monocacy Valley below. The living-dining area would be fitted with a fieldstone fireplace, and a kitchen with a butler's pantry would be constructed on the northeast side of the lodge. Construction began in early May and was completed in time for the president to open it in early July. These photographs show the main lodge in the early stage of construction and in its completed form. (Both, courtesy of Franklin D. Roosevelt Library.)

A unique feature of the landlocked presidential retreat was (and still is) its designation as a US Navy facility. FDR was a former assistant secretary of the Navy and an avid sailor before contracting polio. He therefore had an affinity for all things naval. With the temporary halt in the use of the presidential yacht, many of the staff were redeployed to Shangri La. FDR delightedly designated the retreat the USS Shangri La. He kept a logbook for the new "vessel" and noted on its opening page that the Shangri La was "launched at Catoctin, July 5, 1942." He asked all guests to sign the logbook and termed each visit to the retreat a "cruise." (Both, courtesy of Franklin D. Roosevelt Library.)

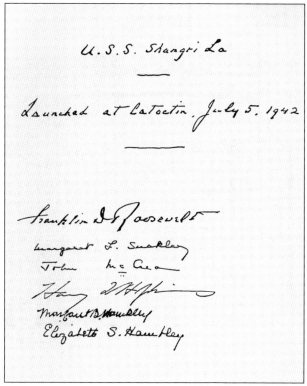

FDR's faithful canine companion, Fala, made himself right at home wherever his master resided. The first pet roamed the White House and Shangri La and frequently posed for photographers. FDR's infirmity from his bout with polio was generally hidden or downplayed, but Fala managed to get himself photographed next to his master's wheelchair (left). He was given his own structure outside the president's lodge (below) and was thoroughly coddled by FDR and his guests. Roosevelt's affection for Fala was well known, particularly after the president playfully complained in a campaign speech that rival Republicans had not only criticized him but had also verbally attacked the innocent Fala. (Both, courtesy of Franklin D. Roosevelt Library.)

FDR thoroughly enjoyed hosting his close staff members and guests at Shangri La. The atmosphere was relaxed, and visitors were encouraged to dress casually. Dinners were generally preceded by a cocktail hour, with FDR often mixing the drinks for staff and guests. Visitors were sometimes invited to bring family members. In the photograph above, taken in November 1942, Catherine (left) and Margaret Hambley, nieces of Margaret Suckley, enjoy breakfast in bed in one of the camp's guest quarters. Margaret "Daisy" Suckley was a distant cousin and close confidante of FDR. (Courtesy of Franklin D. Roosevelt Library.)

FDR spent restful hours at Shangri La working on his stamp collection, playing cards, or simply reading and resting. One of his favorite pastimes was challenging himself to a game of solitaire. The president is pictured here at the dinner table in the main lodge with his signature cigarette perched on a holder jauntily held between his teeth. (Courtesy of Franklin D. Roosevelt Library.)

FDR's guests at Shangri La ranged from heads of state to friends and their families. British prime minister Winston Churchill accompanied the president to the retreat twice. On one occasion, FDR, an avid fisherman, took the prime minister to one of his favorite spots near Shangri La. The two heads of state spent several hours chatting as Churchill smoked a cigar and the president fished. The smoke from the cigar kept the mosquitos at bay, but the president did not catch any fish. (Courtesy of Franklin D. Roosevelt Library.)

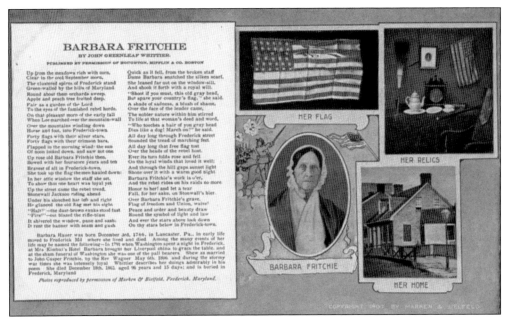

FDR and Churchill's entourage passed through Frederick as it made its way to Shangri La. Churchill, a Civil War buff, was familiar with the legend of Barbara Fritchie and recited from memory the famous poem by John Greenleaf Whittier. On another occasion, the prime minister ventured into the nearby town of Thurmont and stopped at the well-known Cozy Inn for some refreshment. He was fascinated by the jukebox and plunked a few coins in to hear some tunes. (Author's collection.)

Despite the remote location of Shangri La and the many cautions taken to protect the president, security was a major concern. In addition to guarding the entry gate (above), armed Marines patrolled the area around Shangri La when the president was in residence. When the president ventured from the White House, the Secret Service tried to keep his precise movements confidential. Three itineraries were laid out for trips to Camp David. As seen in the communication below for FDR's visit on May 16-17, 1943, the Secret Service's protocol called for deploying agents along the route and maintaining contact throughout the trip. (Both, courtesy of Franklin D. Roosevelt Library.)

> **U. S. SECRET SERVICE**
> **INTER-OFFICE COMMUNICATION**
>
> Confidential
>
> From SA John J. McGrath   Date May 16-17, 1943   File
> To   Chief Frank J. Wilson   Subject Return of the President
>
> May 16 about 7 p.m. received word from SA Reilly that party would return from Shangrala between 10 and 11 a.m., May 17, using Route "C". Contacted Agents Huntington and Stringfellow, using Radio Car 463, and directed them to take up position at Frederick on the morning of the 17th.
>
> May 17 at 10:30 a.m. received word from SA Reilly that party was leaving.
>
> Agents Wildy and Socey assigned to Rockville - Radio Car 452
> Agents Dipper and Fallon - 34th & Mass. Ave. - Radio Car 496
> Agents Raum and Sherbon - Va. Ave. and the Parkway - Radio Car 454
> Agent West - Southwest Gate
>
> At 12:55 p.m. was advised the party had reached The White House.
>
>   John J. McGrath
>   Supervising Agent
>
> JJM:am

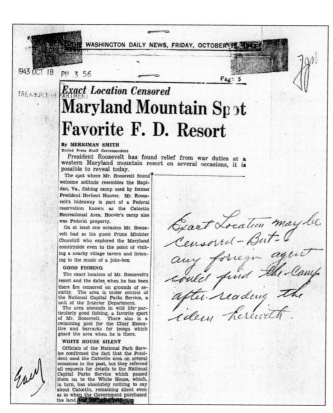

1943 OCT 18 PM 3 56

Page 5

TREASURY DEPARTMENT

Exact Location Censored

Maryland Mountain Spot Favorite F. D. Resort

By MERRIMAN SMITH
United Press Staff Correspondent

President Roosevelt has found relief from war duties at a western Maryland mountain resort on several occasions, it is possible to reveal today.

The spot where Mr. Roosevelt found welcome solitude resembles the Rapidan, Va., fishing camp used by former President Herbert Hoover. Mr. Roosevelt's hideaway is part of a Federal reservation known as the Catoctin Recreational Area. Hoover's camp also was Federal property.

On at least one occasion Mr. Roosevelt had as his guest Prime Minister Churchill who explored the Maryland countryside even to the point of visiting a nearby village tavern and listening to the music of a juke-box.

GOOD FISHING

The exact location of Mr. Roosevelt's resort and the dates when he has been there are censored on grounds of security. The area is under control of the National Capital Parks Service, a unit of the Interior Department.

The area abounds in wild life—particularly good fishing, a favorite sport of Mr. Roosevelt. There also is a swimming pool for the Chief Executive and barracks for troops which guard the area when he is there.

WHITE HOUSE SILENT

Officials of the National Park Service confirmed the fact that the President used the Catoctin area on several occasions in the past, but they referred all requests for details to the National Capital Parks Service which passed them on to the White House, which, in turn, has absolutely nothing to say about Catoctin, remaining silent even as to when the Government purchased the land.

Exact Location may be Censored – But – any foreign agent could find the Camp after reading the idea herewith.

Although local residents were aware of the presidential retreat, the federal government sought to keep its existence as secret as possible. Hence, there was much consternation when, in October 1943, a columnist for the *Washington Daily News* revealed that "President Roosevelt has found relief from war duties at a western Maryland mountain resort . . . part of a Federal reservation known as the Catoctin Recreational Area." (Courtesy of Franklin D. Roosevelt Library.)

Reporters Get Inside View Of Retreat Of Roosevelt

CATOCTIN LODGE OF PRESIDENT

President's Summer Residence Near Thurmont Inspected—Truman Has Never Visited Catoctin Reserve, Guides Say

By ERNEST B. VACCARO

Thurmont, Md., Sept. 30 (AP)—Reporters got an inside view today of historic Shangri La, wartime mountain retreat of Franklin D. Roosevelt.

White House attaches serving as guides in the first public inspection said President Truman has never visited the famous camp.

"Whether he will use it next summer has not been decided, although Mrs. Truman once spent an hour looking it over."

Two thousand feet above the level of the Potomac river in the Catoctin mountains and three miles from this Maryland community, Shangri La is a 70-mile automobile drive from the White House.

Taken Over in 1942

Originally Camp No. 3 in the Catoctin recreational area, built by CCC boys as a part of their national forest work, it was taken over by Mr. Roosevelt in July, 1942, as a weekend spot when the Navy felt it best for him to abandon the use of his yacht for wartime security reasons.

Navy officers said they forbade Mr. Roosevelt to use his yacht for fear of enemy bombing in that critical period of the war.

Medical officers insisted on a spot with a 1,000-foot altitude that

(Continued on Page 2)

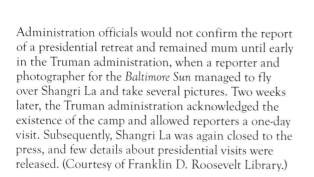

Administration officials would not confirm the report of a presidential retreat and remained mum until early in the Truman administration, when a reporter and photographer for the *Baltimore Sun* managed to fly over Shangri La and take several pictures. Two weeks later, the Truman administration acknowledged the existence of the camp and allowed reporters a one-day visit. Subsequently, Shangri La was again closed to the press, and few details about presidential visits were released. (Courtesy of Franklin D. Roosevelt Library.)

In the months following the death of President Roosevelt, a crew of 20 sailors maintained the grounds and buildings. Authorities in Maryland lobbied for the park to be returned to the state. Finally, in December 1945, it was decided that Shangri La would continue to serve as a presidential retreat. In a letter to the governor of Maryland, President Truman explained, "This action is in accord with the position expressed by the late President Roosevelt before his death." A portion of the park was later returned to the State of Maryland. (Courtesy of National Park Service, Catoctin Mountain Park.)

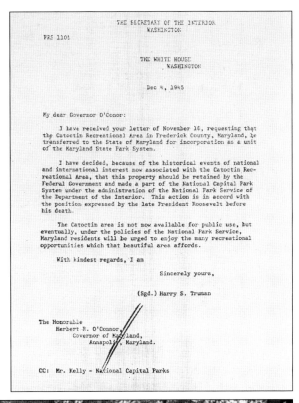

In the tradition established by FDR, Shangri La remained a US Navy facility. Its superintendent is a naval officer, and the responsibilities of maintaining the facilities and serving the president and guests are carried out by naval personnel under his command. The grounds are guarded by US Marines. This staff photograph was taken in September 1950. (Courtesy of Harry S. Truman Library.)

President Truman's longtime getaway spot was a US government-maintained home in Key West dubbed the Little White House. He first visited Shangri La five months after he was thrust unexpectedly into the presidency following FDR's death. Truman found the main lodge confining, with trees and brush crowding the structure. At the request of a top aide, sailors from the presidential yacht were dispatched to create a more open environment by clearing trees and brush from the immediate area. Using local stone, they laid out a spacious patio with a pleasing view of the mountains and countryside. (Courtesy of Harry S. Truman Library.)

Soon after Truman's first visit, the main lodge and some of the cabins were fitted with steam heat, making the compound usable year-round. While the president and his family continued to make frequent use of the Little White House, they also made several visits to Shangri La. Truman's favorite activities at the retreat included long walks and driving himself and guests in the compound's jeep. Bess Truman, while not a big fan of Shangri La, gamely accompanied the president on most of his visits and sometimes hosted old friends and associates. Here, members of Bess's Independence, Missouri, garden club join her for afternoon tea. (Courtesy of Harry S. Truman Library.)

President Truman enjoyed driving and, probably to the consternation of the Secret Service, sometimes insisted on serving as his own driver. These instances were duly recorded in the official President's Daily Diary. For example, an entry for August 8, 1947, noted that at 1:58 p.m., President and Bess Truman headed off to Shangri La with the president at the wheel of his Cadillac convertible. (Courtesy of Harry S. Truman Library.)

Friday, August 8th:

9.45 am   (Honorable Kenneth Royall, Secretary of War)

10.00 am   Cabinet
           (Donaldson for Post Office; Wiggins for Treasury.
           Interior, Agriculture and General Fleming absent.
           All others present)

11.00 am   H.R.H. Sardar Shah Mahmud Khan, the Prime Minister
             of Afghanistan
           (Is in United States on an unofficial visit to see
           his son, who is about to have surgical treatment and
           has, until recently, been a student at Harvard. The
           Prime Minister, who is a brother of the former King
           of Afghanistan and an uncle of the present King,
           has asked for this appointment, thru the State
           Department.)

11.15 am   (Mr. Milton Biow)
           (At the suggestion of Mr. George Killion. Mr. Biow
           has in past been extremely helpful to Democratic
           Party. East Entrance, off record)

11.30 am   (Mr. Frank Pace and father)

12.00   Congressman Cecil R. King, California
           (Phoned Mr. Connelly yesterday for this appointment)

1.00 pm   (Lunch)

1.58 pm   The President, accompanied by Mrs. Truman, departed
           the White House in the convertible Cadillac, with
           the President driving, and motored to "Shangri-La"
           in the Catoctin Mountains, arriving at the main
           lodge at 4.40 p.m.

8.00 pm   The President, accompanied by Mrs. Truman, attended
           a movie, "Carnegie Hall," in the large Navy mess
           hall, after which they returned to their lodge
           and retired for the evening.

Bess Truman was wary of her husband's penchant for fast driving, and as a passenger, reportedly was not shy about ordering him to slow down. When not riding with his wife, the president sometimes drove weekend guests to Shangri La. In this 1949 photograph, Truman is at the wheel with William D. Hassett (presidential secretary) and Joseph Feeney (legislative assistant to the president) as the trio headed to Shangri La. (Courtesy of Harry S. Truman Library.)

Aside from the installation of steam heat, most of the guest cabins remained simple in their furnishings and provisions during the Truman administration. The president permitted staff to use the retreat when he was not there, and it became a well-used year-round venue. The president and staff were required to pay their own expenses. The swimming pool, located about a quarter mile from the main lodge, was a popular attraction. A log with its middle carved out served as a rustic seat from which to enjoy the scenery and the quiet setting of the camp (above). Some of the bedrooms in the cabins had sitting areas and opened directly to the outdoors (below). The stone patio outside the main lodge offered panoramic views of the surrounding countryside as well as a place to relax with a book or a table game. (Both, courtesy of Harry S. Truman Library.)

Three

A NEW NAME

DWIGHT D. EISENHOWER

If Pres. Dwight "Ike" Eisenhower had followed his initial inclination, Shangri La's presidential history would have ended in early 1953. As he noted in a letter to a friend, the new president came into office "committed to an Administration of economy, bordering on or approaching austerity." The retreat in the Catoctin Mountains was, in his view, an unnecessary luxury. The camp, however, was saved from extinction by the entreaties of his attorney general, Herbert Brownell. In May 1953, Brownell and several colleagues visited Shangri La and were so smitten that they drafted a mock "Petition for Executive Clemency." The attorney general, as the "petitioner," argued that the retreat "was convicted without a hearing in the White House . . . and was sentenced to embarrassment, ignominy, and possible obliteration."

The president relented but decided that the name Shangri La was "just a little fancy for a Kansas farm boy." He decided to name the compound after his father and grandson, David. He also renamed the cabins and other facilities at the camp, which during the Roosevelt administration had been given humorous, sometimes tongue-in-cheek names. For example, the main lodge was called The Bear's Den, the communications cabin was One Moment Please, and the physician's quarters was The Pill Box. Eisenhower, with the help of his wife, Mamie, renamed each of the structures after trees and shrubs. The Bear's Den, for example, became Aspen Lodge.

During the Eisenhower administration, Camp David was the scene of meetings with policy advisors, visits with foreign heads of state, and days of simple relaxation for the president and his family.

Among Eisenhower's international visitors were British prime minister Harold MacMillan for discussions about the troubling situation in Berlin, and Soviet head of state Nikita Khrushchev for talks out of which emerged the optimistic but arguably mistaken "spirit of Camp David." Following his heart attack in 1955, Eisenhower recuperated at Camp David and was able to conduct the nation's business through weekly meetings with his cabinet and other officials. The retreat's location only 20 miles from Ike and Mamie's Gettysburg, Pennsylvania, farm allowed the couple to make frequent visits to oversee the construction of their retirement home.

During the eight years of the Eisenhower administration, Camp David was primarily a place where the president enjoyed time with his family, practicing his golf skills, pursuing hobbies such as painting, and simply relaxing.

In his campaign for the presidency, Eisenhower stressed the need for fiscal restraint by the federal government. Accordingly, he seriously considered eliminating Shangri La but was dissuaded by several top officials. Ike visited the retreat and decided to keep "the little camp up in the Catoctins." In the photograph at left, he is seen coming out of the presidential lodge on his way to fish at a nearby creek. Below, the president is enjoying some angling success. (Left, courtesy of Dwight D. Eisenhower Library; below, courtesy of National Park Service, Catoctin Mountain Park.)

On September 15, 1959, Soviet leader Nikita Khrushchev arrived in Washington for an extended tour of the United States, culminating in meetings with Eisenhower at Camp David. Khrushchev was at first wary of meeting at the presidential retreat because neither he nor his staff knew many details about the rustic site or what, if anything, an invitation signified. The two leaders engaged in extensive discussions, interspersed with long walks and a viewing of popular Western films. The talks were difficult but ultimately ended on a relatively positive note, which was characterized, perhaps mistakenly, as the spirit of Camp David. Ironically, the Soviet leader was probably unaware that he was at times standing over the camp's recently completed bomb shelter. (Both, courtesy of Dwight D. Eisenhower Library.)

Ike hosted several heads of state at Camp David during his presidency. In addition to Khrushchev, Eisenhower's foreign guests included Pres. Charles De Gaulle of France (above), Pres. Adolfo Lopez Mateo of Mexico, and Pres. Alberto Lleras Camargo of Colombia. During these visits, Ike often invited his guests to join him in viewing movies at the camp's rustic "theater." The choice of movies primarily reflected Ike's love of Westerns. British prime minister Harold Macmillan, during his visit in 1959 to discuss the Berlin situation (below), sat stoically through these "inconceivably banal" films. (Both, courtesy of Dwight D. Eisenhower Library.)

While on many occasions President Eisenhower conducted official business at Camp David, he also viewed the retreat as a place to relax and temporarily escape from the daily pressures of the nation's capital. At the camp, he was able to spend some "alone" time with Mamie and could pursue hobbies, such as painting and cooking, with few interruptions. In the image above, Ike and Mamie are playing a game of Scrabble on the patio of the presidential lodge. Ike was a talented artist and enjoyed honing his skills during spare time at Camp David (right) and at his Gettysburg farm during his retirement years. (Both, courtesy of Dwight D. Eisenhower Library.)

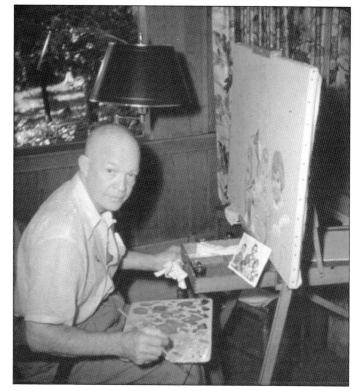

Eisenhower was an avid golfer. During his tenure, a three-hole golf course was laid out near the presidential lodge. It was designed by renowned golf course designer Robert Trent Jones as a miniature version of Eisenhower's favorite courses—Burning Tree and Augusta National. In this photograph, Ike is giving a golf lesson to his grandson David. (Courtesy of Dwight D. Eisenhower Library.)

Ike and Mamie were devoted grandparents and often spent time with the grandchildren at Camp David. Among the many things to do at the camp were bowling, card games, a playground, and of course, learning to play golf. In this photograph, Mamie and Ike are surrounded by, from left to right, Susan, David, and Anne Eisenhower. (Courtesy of Dwight D. Eisenhower Library.)

On September 23, 1955, President Eisenhower suffered a heart attack. He recuperated at Camp David, and on November 21 was able to host a brief meeting of his National Security Council. The following day, his cabinet members journeyed to the camp for the first of what became weekly meetings at the retreat. Ike stayed for an hour and later reported that "I felt no fatigue or weariness and concluded that I would soon resume the daily work schedule to which I was accustomed." (Courtesy of Dwight D. Eisenhower Library.)

Vice Pres. Richard Nixon (left), of course, attended the weekly meetings and visited the presidential retreat on several other occasions. He was not an avid fisherman; in this photograph, he is taking a few fishing pointers from his boss. (Courtesy of Dwight D. Eisenhower Library.)

When Shangri La was created in 1942, the 65-mile trip through rolling hills and towns took up to two hours by car. The car in which the president rode was always accompanied by Secret Service vehicles. Agents were also deployed along the route to ensure the safety of the president. If the entourage's route went through Frederick, the trip was slowed by cars, people, and traffic lights. This procedure was followed during the Truman administration and into the first years of Eisenhower's presidency. The entry gate to Camp David during the Eisenhower administration is pictured above. In 1957, Eisenhower became the first president to travel to Shangri La/Camp David by helicopter. This reduced the travel time to about 30 minutes and provided greater security. The helicopter was a two-seat Bell Ranger, chosen because of its safety record. Eisenhower was accompanied on the inaugural flight by the chief of his Secret Service detail. The Bell Ranger was soon replaced for trips to Camp David by a larger military transport helicopter. (Above, courtesy of Dwight D. Eisenhower Library; below, courtesy of Thurmont Images.)

Four

NEW FRONTIER AND GREAT SOCIETY
JFK AND LBJ

Pres. John F. Kennedy had a wide choice of places for his family to vacation, and Camp David did not top his list. In addition to the Kennedy family compound in Hyannis Port, Massachusetts, there was Jackie's uncle's farm in Newport, Rhode Island; the Kennedys' winter home in Palm Beach, Florida; and the estate, Glen Ora, that he and Jackie had recently leased in Middleburg, Virginia.

JFK's first visit to Camp David was not for relaxation. In April 1961, a small brigade of Cuban emigres, backed by the US government, landed in the island's Bay of Pigs to spark a revolution against the government of Fidel Castro. The resulting debacle was a deep embarrassment to the new US administration. Consequently, JFK asked his predecessor—former five-star general Dwight D. Eisenhower—to meet with him at Camp David to share his expertise and experience to ensure that the Bay of Pigs calamity was never repeated.

JFK visited Camp David only twice more in his first two years in office. In 1963, while a new home was under construction in Virginia, the family began spending time at Camp David. They enjoyed the quiet, secure mountain location and began spending weekends at the camp. Jackie brought her horses to the retreat and asked that a pony ring be set up for Caroline. JFK was able to live a semblance of a normal life when he was there, sleeping late, playing with his children, practicing his swing on the small golf course, and using many of the other recreational facilities. Jackie was even able to take occasional shopping trips to Thurmont without being mobbed by the press.

JFK and the family visited Camp David 16 times during 1963, including his final visit six weeks before his tragic death.

Kennedy's successor, Lyndon B. Johnson, first traveled to the camp on a snowy day in January 1964. There he was introduced to bowling, a sport he had never tried. On his first roll, he knocked down seven pins. Not satisfied, he continued until he bowled a strike.

While LBJ found time to relax at Camp David, he stayed in close touch with his advisors and spent at least a part of most days working. He enjoyed walking around the camp but, true to his restless nature, generally at a rapid pace. Other favorite activities included swimming and watching movies (although he often fell asleep during showings).

Lady Bird Johnson found the mountain location charming and appreciated the rare quiet the retreat afforded the first family. LBJ's daughters were fond of the camp and often brought along friends.

President Johnson and Lady Bird visited Camp David 29 times during his time in office but preferred their own LBJ Ranch in Texas. The president treated the ranch as a second workplace, leading the press to dub it "The Texas White House."

When JFK took office in 1961, he and Jackie made it clear that they did not intend to make much use of Camp David. In addition to their homes at Hyannis Port (above) and Palm Beach, they had rented a villa in Virginia hunt country. When the lease on the latter ran out in 1963, the Kennedys began spending more time at Camp David. The family compound at Hyannis Port sits on six acres of waterfront property. (Courtesy of Michael Gwyther-Jones.)

The Kennedy family purchased their Palm Beach home in 1933 from Rodman Wannamaker, owner of the famous Philadelphia department store that carried the family name. In 1956, while recovering from back surgery at the Palm Beach home, JFK wrote his Pulitzer Prize–winning book *Profiles in Courage*. In November 1963, the president and his family spent the weekend at the estate before the fateful trip to Dallas. The home sits on an acre of waterfront land and is no longer owned by the Kennedys. (Courtesy of Department of Commerce.)

In April 1961, following the disastrous Bay of Pigs invasion by US-supported Cuban exiles, JFK invited former president Eisenhower to Camp David. Kennedy sought the advice of his predecessor and assured Ike that he would never again engage in such a venture without a plan that would ensure success. (Courtesy of Dwight D. Eisenhower Library.)

As is evident in this photograph, the meeting of the current and former presidents was a major story. President Kennedy went to the helicopter landing area to greet the former five-star general. The press corps was granted entry to the landing site to cover the event. (Courtesy of John F. Kennedy Library.)

Aspen has been the presidential lodge since the inception of the camp in 1942. Originally dubbed The Bear's Den by FDR, it was renamed Aspen Lodge during the Eisenhower administration as a tribute to Mamie's home state of Colorado. It rests on a three-acre clearing with a panoramic view of the countryside. In the years leading up to the Kennedy administration, the lodge underwent a number of alterations, including a second patio, additional bathrooms, and air-conditioning. By 1961, the original rustic combination of three small cabins in one had become a very inviting and comfortable dwelling. (Courtesy of John F. Kennedy Library.)

Camp David was guarded by a squadron of armed, uniformed US Marines. Jackie was concerned that the constant proximity of soldiers with guns would have a deleterious effect on Caroline and John Jr. Consequently, the civilian-clothed Secret Service detail provided security for the children at the camp. In this photograph, Caroline is enjoying the company of Secret Service agent Bob Foster. (Courtesy John F. Kennedy Library.)

The first son was two years old when the family began spending frequent weekends at Camp David after the termination of the lease on the Glen Ora home. He was known as "John-John" by the general public, a name he mistakenly acquired when a reporter heard JFK calling him John twice in succession. Much to the delight of the young presidential son, the family most often traveled to the retreat by helicopter. In the photograph at right, John-John is having a grand time piloting the presidential helicopter. Below, he awaits the landing of his father's helicopter. (Both, courtesy of John F. Kennedy Library.)

In 1963, while their home in Middleburg was under construction, the Kennedys made frequent use of Camp David. Jackie, an avid horsewoman, had her horses moved to the camp. A pony ring was laid out for Caroline and other young visitors. In March 1963, the family spent a weekend horseback riding and relaxing at Camp David. In the photograph above, Caroline is atop her favorite pony, Macaroni. Below, President Kennedy is walking with two-and-a-half-year-old John-John near the stables. (Both, courtesy of John F. Kennedy Library.)

When Shangri La was created in 1942, the cabins were unheated, and the retreat lay dormant during the winter. Steam heat was installed in the president's lodge and several of the cabins during Truman's tenure, making it possible for the camp to remain open year-round. Snowfall turned the camp and its surroundings into a winter wonderland. The photograph above captures the beauty of a winter day during the Kennedy and Johnson years. (Courtesy of John F. Kennedy Library.)

While President Johnson enjoyed the convenience and atmosphere of Camp David, he traveled as often as possible to his "true home," his ranch at Stonewall, Texas. At the time of LBJ's presidency, the 2,700-acre ranch was home to 400 head of registered Hereford cattle. The main house was 8,400 square feet and had eight bedrooms and nine bathrooms. LBJ returned to the ranch after his presidency and lived there until his death in 1973. (Courtesy of National Park Service.)

45

Johnson's five years in office were marked by several significant issues, including race relations and voting rights legislation, the creation of Medicare and Medicaid, turmoil in the Dominican Republic, the Six-Day War in the Middle East, student unrest in the United States, and of course, the escalating war in Vietnam. Camp David often served as a place for Johnson to deliberate and hold meetings with his advisors. In the above image, the photographer offers a glimpse through a window of Johnson engaged in a dinner meeting with members of his national security team. Seated at the table are, from left to right, Marvin Watson (often called LBJ's unofficial chief of staff), McGeorge Bundy (national security adviser), Bill Moyers (White House press secretary), Secretary of State Dean Rusk, President Johnson, Secretary of Defense Robert McNamara, and Jack Valenti (special assistant). (Courtesy of Lyndon B. Johnson Library.)

Lady Bird Johnson described the quiet seclusion of Camp David as "an insulation that keeps you from being terribly worried about what's going on in the outside world." Occasionally, she could reign in her workaholic husband and simply take a relaxing stroll. (Courtesy of Lyndon B. Johnson Library.)

The pace of life for presidents often seems nonstop. In June 1967, LBJ and Lady Bird Johnson hosted a weekend at Camp David with Australian prime minister Harold Holt and his wife, Zara. The President's Daily Diary notes that he was in Texas the day before their arrival and flew at midnight on Air Force One to Washington. He had breakfast in the White House at 10:00 a.m., and over the next four hours had seven meetings with cabinet members and staff. At 1:56 p.m., he helicoptered to Dulles Airport to meet the prime minister and his party. They proceeded to Camp David, arrived at 2:36 p.m., and spent the afternoon at the swimming pool (above). The president then changed and met with the prime minister before the evening's formal dinner (below). W. Dale Nelson, in his book about Camp David, recounts that Holt had not brought a bathing suit on the trip and borrowed one from LBJ. President Johnson was a large man, and his swimming trunks fit a bit loosely on the prime minister. As a result, the suit came undone on Holt's first dive. (Both, courtesy of Lyndon B. Johnson Library.)

The war in Vietnam was a prime concern during the LBJ presidency. In April 1968, Johnson gathered top officials in his administration at Camp David to discuss strategy and policy. One of the president's favorite pastimes at Camp David was driving his Lincoln Continental convertible. As seen in the photograph above, he motored to the helipad to pick up the participants. Yuki, one of the president's dogs, accompanied him and leaped onto the car's trunk to greet the guests. Later in the day, Johnson and his ambassador to Vietnam, Ellsworth Bunker, conversed by the pond near the Aspen Lodge (left). (Both, courtesy of Lyndon B. Johnson Library.)

Five

ABBREVIATED TENURES
RICHARD NIXON AND GERALD FORD

When he took office in 1969, Richard Nixon was no stranger to Camp David. As vice president under Dwight Eisenhower, he had visited the retreat several times. In contrast to the casual clothing he was sometimes seen wearing during these visits, Nixon rarely was without coat and tie at the camp during his own administration.

This stiff, serious demeanor accurately reflected President Nixon's activities during most of his visits to Camp David. He rarely used the recreational facilities at the retreat, preferring to spend his time in quiet reflection, writing speeches, and meeting with his domestic and foreign policy advisors. He found the remote, quiet surroundings a welcome escape from the constant day-to-day interactions and interruptions of life in the White House. Many of his most notable speeches and writings were crafted at Camp David, including his eulogy at Eisenhower's funeral, a major Vietnam policy address in 1969, and several State of the Union addresses. Late in his administration, as he struggled with the fallout from the Watergate fiasco and his ultimate decision to resign, Nixon spent many days at the retreat pondering his fate.

Camp David was also a favored site for meetings with foreign heads of state. During Soviet leader Leonid Brezhnev's state visit in June 1973, the two leaders spent time at Camp David. Nixon's daughters, Tricia and Julie, hosted an evening at the retreat for Princess Anne and Prince Charles of the United Kingdom.

By the time Nixon left office, he had logged 160 trips to Camp David, significantly more than any of his predecessors.

In contrast to Nixon's subdued personality and propensity toward spending quiet days at Camp David, Pres. Gerald Ford's approach was upbeat and vigorous. While he did conduct business on virtually all his visits, President Ford found time to take ample advantage of the recreational facilities available at the retreat.

During his 30 months in office, Ford visited Camp David 29 times. He held several important meetings at the camp on the economy, energy, trade, and housing. He hosted only one foreign leader during this period—President Suharto of Indonesia.

During Ford's term of office, his wife, Betty, was diagnosed and treated for breast cancer. She visited the retreat a month after leaving the hospital. Camp David, in her view, was "the best thing about the White House." The president shared her fondness for the camp, noting that it is "a place where you can really live as a family."

President Nixon spent more time at Camp David than all his predecessors combined. By the time he took office in 1969, much of the camp was in serious need of renovation. While each president before him made some changes to the facilities, the cabins were beginning to show signs of aging and a bit of neglect. One of the major changes was the construction of a new swimming pool close to the presidential lodge (above). The previous pool was constructed in the 1930s and was situated about a quarter mile from the main cabin. The layout of the new pool placed it directly above the bomb shelter built during the Eisenhower administration. Other changes to the camp included the construction of a large, modern lodge to house offices and facilities for conferences (below). It was named Laurel and replaced an older cabin with the same name. The new facility has three conference rooms, a kitchen, large dining hall, and a small office for the president. Two guest cabins, Maple and Red Oak, were built during the Nixon administration to improve and expand the existing facilities. (Both, courtesy of Richard Nixon Library.)

Nixon purchased the property that became "The Western White House" shortly after assuming the presidency. The Spanish-style home—La Casa Pacifica—was in San Clemente, California, on a bluff overlooking the Pacific Ocean. During his time in office, the president used the estate for working vacations. He also hosted visits by several foreign leaders. (Courtesy of Richard Nixon Library.)

While many of the traditional Nixon family get-togethers took place at the president's home in San Clemente or his "Florida White House" in Key Biscayne, the president and his family sometimes celebrated milestones at Camp David. Here, the family is gathered in June 1970 to mark multiple graduations: Julie from Smith College, her fiancé David Eisenhower from Amherst College, and Susan Eisenhower from the Westtown School. (Courtesy of Richard Nixon Library.)

The courtship and marriage of Julie Nixon and David Eisenhower solidified the link between the two presidential families after the close of the Eisenhower administration and the death of the former president in 1969. Mamie Eisenhower was an honored member of the extended family. In this photograph, the clan is gathered at Camp David in 1971 to celebrate Mamie's 77th birthday. (Courtesy of Richard Nixon Library.)

David Eisenhower and Julie Nixon were married on December 22, 1968. The newlyweds spent their honeymoon at Camp David. They had met as eight-year-olds and are pictured here at the presidential swearing-in ceremony for David's grandfather, Dwight D. Eisenhower, in 1957. The couple chose to be married in New York to avoid the intense publicity of a White House wedding. (Courtesy of Richard Nixon Library.)

Nixon seemed to truly enjoy the "uncharged" atmosphere of Camp David. Here, he was able to think and write with relatively few interruptions (above). He wrote several major speeches during visits to the retreat, including State of the Union and policy addresses. Beset with major crises such as the Vietnam war and later, the fallout from the Watergate break-in, the president found the camp a welcome refuge and a place where he could contemplate plans to deal with these and other troubling issues. During his second term, Nixon spent increasing amounts of time at the camp in relative isolation with no meetings or advisors (below). (Both, courtesy of Richard Nixon Library.)

Unlike his predecessors, President Nixon rarely dressed casually at Camp David. In December 1971, he posed for several photographs in what may have been an effort to counter his rather stiff image. For this photograph, he donned a Camp David jacket and leaned casually on one of the split rail fences at the retreat. (Courtesy of Richard Nixon Library.)

The president and his wife, Pat, often brought their dogs to the camp. In this photograph, the first couple are walking all three canines, Vicky, Pasha, and King Timahoe, along one of Camp David's paths. Note the formal attire. (Courtesy of Richard Nixon Library.)

Ronald Reagan (above, right) and George H.W. Bush (below, center) each spent time with Nixon at Camp David. While it is not clear if either harbored presidential ambitions at the time of their visits, they turned out to be two of the most prolific users of the retreat during their terms in office. At the time of Reagan's visit in August 1972, he was serving as governor of California, a post he held until 1975. Bush was Nixon's ambassador to the United Nations from 1971 to 1973. (Both, courtesy of Richard Nixon Library.)

During his first term in office, Nixon often hosted meetings with his advisors and cabinet at Camp David. Domestic topics included welfare reform, wage and price restraints, the environment, and the economy. Vietnam and Southeast Asia dominated the discussions on international affairs. The cabinet meeting in the above photograph took place at the Laurel Lodge in August 1969. Nixon is seated at center on the right side of the table. The larger meetings at Camp David tapered off during Nixon's second term and were confined primarily to discussions with a small group of his closest aides. Below, the president is discussing the situation in Vietnam in November 1973 with Secretary of State Henry Kissinger (left) and White House chief of staff Alexander Haig. (Both, courtesy of Richard Nixon Library.)

President Nixon found Camp David to be an excellent venue for discussions with foreign heads of state. Over the years since its founding, an invitation to visit the retreat had become a special honor not routinely accorded to all visiting foreign leaders. In October 1971, Yugoslav prime minister Tito and his wife, Jovanka, were invited to visit Camp David. Tito was a World War II hero who notably later led his country out of the Soviet Union's sphere of influence. In the photograph above, Tito is viewing the Catoctin scenery as Jovanka looks on. Below, Nixon is walking the grounds with British prime minister Edward Heath in December 1970. (Both, courtesy of Richard Nixon Library.)

In June 1973, Soviet Communist Party general secretary Leonid Brezhnev traveled to the United States on a state visit to discuss nuclear arms and other pressing issues. He was taken first to Camp David where he remained for two days to get acclimated and unwind before meeting with Nixon. The two met in Washington, and two days later traveled to Camp David to continue the talks. There, Nixon presented his guest with a Camp David jacket. (Courtesy of Richard Nixon Library.)

Knowing of Brezhnev's fondness for automobiles, Nixon presented the general secretary with a dark blue 1973 Lincoln Continental donated by the Ford Motor Company. Brezhnev asked Nixon to join him for a test drive. The Soviet leader took the wheel and proceeded to spin around the winding roads at speeds up to 50 miles per hour. After a hair-raising ride that included several hairpin turns, Brezhnev told the shaken president, "This is a very fine automobile. It holds the road well." (Courtesy of Richard Nixon Library.)

Gerald Ford's first weeks in the White House were marked by his pardon of former president Richard Nixon, an appearance before a joint session of Congress, a visit by King Hussein of Jordan, and the selection of Nelson Rockefeller to be his vice president. Following these exhausting weeks, a visit with his family to Camp David from August 31 to September 2 must have been much welcomed. The Ford family seemed eager to try most of the recreational activities that the retreat offered. In the above photograph, the president is working on his swing at the small three-hole golf course. Below, he is testing out the camp's trampoline as daughter Susan watches. (Both, courtesy of Gerald Ford Library.)

One of the first visitors to Camp David after the Ford family arrived was a fawn named Flag, who seems to have easily won the affections of the new stewards of the presidential retreat. Pictured with the president and his wife are two of their children, son Steve and daughter Susan. (Courtesy of Gerald Ford Library.)

The Fords often made use of the camp's swimming pool when weather permitted. In this photograph, it is evident that the first dog, Liberty, shared the family's fondness for water sports. (Courtesy of Gerald Ford Library.)

President Ford retained many of Nixon's senior advisors following the latter's resignation. The new president faced serious domestic and international issues and utilized the experience of officials he knew and had worked with during his brief time as Nixon's vice president. His visits to Camp David were filled with a mix of discussions with advisors and relaxation time. In this photograph, the president is meeting at the retreat with his secretary of state, Henry Kissinger. (Courtesy of Gerald Ford Library.)

Ford's only foreign guest at Camp David was President Suharto of Indonesia, in July 1975. The two leaders and their delegations met for a working lunch on the patio of Laurel Lodge, followed by talks inside between the two heads of state. Among the matters discussed were the situation in Vietnam following the US withdrawal and the goals of the USSR and China in Southeast Asia. (Courtesy of Gerald Ford Library.)

Ford had been the congressional representative for his Michigan district for 25 years when he was chosen by Nixon to replace Spiro Agnew as vice president. His reputation as a down-to-earth family man followed him to the White House. He enjoyed interacting with the personnel who served him, and was well-liked and respected by them. In the above photograph, the president is chatting with some of the Navy personnel at their Camp David mess hall. (Courtesy of Gerald Ford Library.)

The Fords were avid skiers and spent most of their winter vacations at the Vail ski resort in Colorado. On brief winter jaunts to Camp David, however, snowmobiling was a favorite activity. It appears from this photograph that the first dog shared their enthusiasm. (Courtesy of Gerald Ford Library.)

Although most vacations were spent away from the Washington, DC, area, the family sometimes gathered at Camp David to celebrate a holiday. Thanksgiving 1976 was one of those occasions, and as seen in the photograph, the president was assigned carving duties. (Courtesy of Gerald Ford Library.)

Following Richard Nixon's resignation, Ford served as president for the remaining 895 days of his predecessor's administration. In 1976, Ford decided to seek election to his own full term of office. His campaign staff met at Camp David in August 1976 to discuss strategy for the upcoming race. (Courtesy of Gerald Ford Library.)

Despite the pressures of the office during his days as president, Ford was careful to set aside time to be with his wife and family. In the photograph above, he and the first lady are relaxing in the living quarters at Aspen, the presidential lodge at Camp David. Below, daughter Susan has landed a piggyback ride from the president during some family horseplay at the retreat. (Courtesy of Gerald Ford Library.)

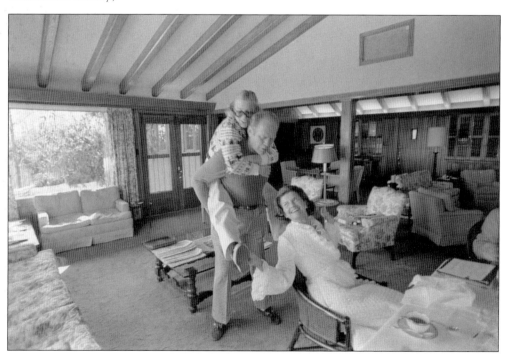

Six

PEACEMAKING

JIMMY CARTER

Pres. Jimmy Carter and family members were frequent visitors to Camp David. While the retreat provided a means of welcome respite from the pressures of White House life, it also served as the venue for Carter's historic achievement—brokering a peace agreement between Israel and Egypt in 1978.

One month after his inauguration, the president; his wife, Roslyn; and daughter Amy made their first visit to the camp. They tried out many of its recreational offerings, including swimming, biking, and bowling, and became frequent visitors. Carter traveled to Camp David 99 times and stayed for 277 days during his four years in office.

While he made ample use of the camp's facilities, the president spent a significant portion of time hosting domestic and international meetings and discussing policy with his senior advisors. Of the two most memorable negotiations, one—the talks leading to the Camp David Accords—was a major success, while the other—the domestic summit of 1979—was disappointing.

The Middle East negotiations actually began at Camp David several months before the Egyptian and Israeli delegations came together for their historic talks. In February 1978, President Carter invited Egyptian president Anwar Sadat and his wife to join him and Roslyn for a weekend at Camp David. The two couples enjoyed quiet walks, relaxed dinners, and rides around the grounds on Golf Cart One. Most significantly, the two presidents engaged in what turned out to be preliminary talks leading to the momentous days of the Camp David Summit later in the year.

The other major set of meetings the president convened at Camp David focused on domestic affairs. In July 1979, Carter held discussion sessions with groups of governors, local government leaders, congressmen, senators, business executives, labor leaders, economists, energy experts, and political advisors in an effort to formulate policies to deal with issues affecting domestic life in the United States. He followed up these sessions with personal visits to several areas around the country. Ultimately, the president's efforts to address and resolve many major domestic issues were unsuccessful.

During his final months in office, faced with the Iran hostage crisis and other difficult issues at home and abroad, Carter continued to find a degree of solace in regular visits to the Catoctin Mountain retreat at Camp David.

President Carter was very much a family man. Roslyn and Amy Carter generally accompanied him to Camp David, and he was careful to balance his work schedule with family time. Amy sometimes brought a friend to the camp. On a snowy day in February 1979, the president served as the children's pack horse on a sledding expedition around the hills of the camp (above). Later that day, the family mounted cross-country skis and traveled to nearby Camp Greentop for an afternoon on the snowy hills (below). (Both, courtesy of Jimmy Carter Library.)

As with many presidential wives, Roslyn served without pay as the president's closest advisor, partner in diplomacy, and devoted companion. She was present and active at the most momentous times and during periods of crisis in Carter's term of office. In the photograph at right, the president and first lady are walking to the helicopter that will carry them back to the White House after a visit to Camp David. (Courtesy of Jimmy Carter Library.)

Amy Carter, the first daughter, was a lively presence during the Carter presidency. Her demonstrative love of reading was well noted in press photographs of her at dinners and other functions. The president and Roslyn Carter strived to create an environment in which Amy could experience a "normal" childhood. This photograph makes clear that she was daddy's little girl. Note that Misty Malarky, Amy's cat, has made his way into the picture. (Courtesy of Jimmy Carter Library.)

From	To	PHONE P=Placed R=Rec'd	ACTIVITY
8:31	8:36	P	The President talked with his Assistant for National Security Affairs, Zbigniew Brzezinski.
			The President went to Laurel Lodge.
10:00	1:00		The President met to discuss the economy with economic, labor and business leaders. For a list of attendees, see APPENDIX "A."
			The Presidential party had lunch.
12:35		R	The President was telephoned by Deputy Secretary of Defense Charles W. Duncan, Jr. The call was not completed.
			The President returned to Aspen Lodge.
1:02		R	The President was telephoned by Harold S. Gulliver, Jr., Editor of the Atlanta Constitution, Atlanta, Georgia. The call was not completed.
2:51	2:53	R	The President talked with his Press Secretary, Joseph L. "Jody" Powell.
4:01	4:05	P	The President talked with Vice President Walter F. Mondale.
4:05	4:10	P	The President talked with Deputy Secretary Duncan.
4:11	4:15	P	The President talked with his Assistant for Domestic Affairs and Policy, Stuart E. Eizenstat.
4:16	4:19	P	The President talked with Representative Dan Rostenkowski (D-Illinois).
4:20	4:21	P	The President talked with Vice President Mondale.
4:39	4:43	R	The President talked with his Assistant for Congressional Liaison, Frank B. Moore.
4:44	4:45	P	The President talked with his Assistant, Hamilton Jordan.
4:48	4:54	P	The President talked with Chairman of the Council of Economic Advisers (CEA) Charles L. Schultze.

The detailed activities of presidents are recorded in a log called the President's Daily Diary. While President Carter strove to mix relaxation with business while at Camp David, there were many days when the nation's business left little time for rest or recreation. For example, on July 10, 1979, Carter held a meeting with economic, labor, and business leaders and conferred with the vice president, other cabinet officers, his congressional affairs assistant, the chairman of the Council of Economic Advisors, and a senior congressman. (Courtesy of Jimmy Carter Library.)

When domestic and world events allowed, Sundays were primarily days of worship and recreation. This memo outlining the president's activities notes that on March 2, 1980, Carter and family attended worship services in the morning and went cross-country skiing in the afternoon. (Courtesy of Jimmy Carter Library.)

THE WHITE HOUSE
WASHINGTON
March 4, 1980

MEMORANDUM FOR   NELL YATES

FROM   JOSE MURATTI

SUBJECT   Presidential Activities

Friday, February 29, 1980

3:45 p.m.   The President accompanied by Chip Carter and James E. Carter IV boarded Marine One and departed for Camp David.

4:22 p.m.   Marine One arrived at Camp David. The President proceeded to Aspen Lodge on foot.

              The Neil Goldschmidt family (4 persons) arrived by private auto early in the evening.

Saturday, March 1, 1980

              Amy Carter and Kathy Wolfe arrived by motorcade during the morning.
              Movie "My Brilliant Career"
              FL, Chip, Amy + Staff

Sunday, March 2, 1980

10:00 a.m.   The President, Mrs. Carter, Chip, James IV, Amy and Kathy Wolfe attended religious services conducted by Chaplain Ray Woodall at Hickory Lodge.

10:30 a.m.   Services concluded.

11:00 a.m.   The President, Mrs. Carter, Chip, Amy, Kathy Wolfe, Dr. Lukash, Phil Wise and Major Muratti departed by motorcade for cross-country skiing at Greentop Lodge area.

12:30 p.m.   Picnic lunch served at Greentop Lodge.

1:00 p.m.   Lunch concluded. The President and his party proceeded by motorcade to Camp David for further skiing.

3:00 p.m.   Skiing concluded.

4:30 p.m.   Mrs. Carter, Chip, James IV, Amy and Kathy departed by motorcade for Wasington, D.C.

              movie "Barry Lyndon"
              w/staff

Following the establishment of the State of Israel in 1948, four US administrations tried unsuccessfully to broker peace between the new country and its Arab neighbors. Early in the Carter administration, the president and his advisors initiated steps aimed at promoting this objective. In November 1977, Egyptian president Anwar Sadat made a bold, unprecedented visit to Israel. Three months later, President Carter invited Sadat and his wife to visit Camp David. The president and Roslyn enjoyed an amiable weekend with the Sadats. The two presidents discussed Egyptian-Israeli relations and the possibility of bringing the two nations together for talks aimed at finding a path to peace. Six months later, the two sides met at Camp David for historic talks brokered by Carter. (Both, courtesy of Jimmy Carter Library.)

Archery
Horsesh
Volleyba
Badmint

Maple

Hickory

Poplar
- Camp office

Dogwood

Aspen Lodge

Birch

Cedar
- Camp Commander's house

Witch Hazel

Rosebud

At the Camp David Summit, the president and his advisors carefully assigned cabins to the leaders of the two sides and their advisors. Prime Minister Begin was housed in the Birch cabin and President Sadat was lodged in the Dogwood cabin. The two dwellings are set in shady areas and, strategically, are equidistant from each other and the president's Aspen Lodge, as seen here. Many of the discussions during the days leading up to the accord took place in the large meeting room in the Holly cabin. Senior staff members of each delegation were quartered in cabins around the retreat; because of the large numbers of advisors, they often had to double up in rooms. (Google Maps.)

President Carter believed the talks would last several days, but no longer than a week. At several points in the discussions, it appeared that one or the other of the Egyptian and Israeli leaders would give up in anger or frustration and withdraw from the negotiations. On each of these occasions, Carter and senior staff members successfully kept the talks going. (Courtesy of Jimmy Carter Library.)

The little town of Thurmont became an important world center for the 13 days of the Camp David Summit. Reporters and other media personnel were headquartered at the town's American Legion Hall, and many stayed at the Cozy Inn, the restaurant made famous by Winston Churchill's beer and jukebox visit in 1943. Note the mobile communication tower and the Cozy catering truck. (Courtesy of Thurmont Main.)

The president and his staff felt that a key to success would be to include some relaxed activities along with the serious and delicate negotiations. In the photograph above, Prime Minister Begin (left) is engrossed in a chess game with President Carter's national security advisor, Zbigniew Brzezinski. The negotiations were often mercurial, marked by threats to end the talks and leave. There were, however, amicable encounters, as seen in the photograph below of a meeting between the two leaders and their delegations. (Both, courtesy of Jimmy Carter Library.)

Seven

THE GIPPER

RONALD REAGAN

President Reagan and his wife, Nancy, regularly set sail on "the good ship Camp David" during the two terms of the Reagan administration. The president's advisors feared that the many days he spent at Camp David (571 days during 187 visits) would lead to a public perception of laziness and inattention to his job. This was compounded by frequent visits to his California ranch (345 days). Nevertheless, the president was not swayed from what he believed to be a mental and physical necessity. While he did engage in job-related work, he was able to truly relax and enjoy the beauty of the surroundings and the recreational activities available at the camp. He and Nancy kept guest visits to a minimum and shared many hours of walks, movie viewing, and their favorite pastime—horseback riding.

The president made good use of his vaunted communication skills by inaugurating brief weekly radio broadcasts to outline domestic and foreign policies and issues. While earlier presidents used Camp David as a venue for visits by world leaders, Reagan hosted only three heads of state at the retreat during his eight years in office. He met with cabinet officers and advisors and hosted several meetings with congressional leaders but kept these to a minimum, preferring to conduct official business primarily in Washington when possible.

Not surprisingly, given their backgrounds as professional actors, President Reagan and the first lady thoroughly enjoyed viewing movies in the Aspen Lodge's mini theater room. It was a rare weekend that the president and Nancy did not watch at least one movie. When guests were present, the president enjoyed sharing stories from his Hollywood years.

In the days leading up to Reagan's first-term inauguration, Pat Nixon told Nancy Reagan that "without Camp David, you'll go stir crazy." Nancy validated that view when, in an interview for a book on her husband, she noted that "it was so important to us, in keeping our perspective on things, to be able to be there alone, to have quiet time together to think and reflect and get our thoughts in order."

The Reagan family's favorite recreational activity was horseback riding. The president and Nancy rode often at Camp David and their ranch in California. The stables at the camp that had been erected during the Kennedy administration had long been removed, and under President Nixon, the trails had been paved over. The Secret Service set up a small stable near the helicopter pad and brought in horses from the outside when the president was in residence. The Secret Service tried to keep a respectable distance behind the Reagans to allow them some solitude, but the agents carried communication equipment and were always on alert. Fittingly, Reagan's code name was "Rawhide." Nancy's was "Rainbow." Reagan reportedly pressed the outer range of the rides, and the route was gradually extended. (Courtesy of Ronald Reagan Library.)

President Reagan and the first lady created a relaxed atmosphere at Camp David, dressing in jeans or riding gear and keeping as low a profile as possible. As commander in chief, Reagan had to tolerate a bit of pomp, as illustrated in the above photograph. He enjoyed occasional interactions with the "crew" of the USS Camp David. Below, he and Nancy have lunch with the military personnel at their mess. (Both, courtesy of Ronald Reagan Library.)

Soon after Reagan assumed the presidency, Camp David became a regular weekend retreat for the president and first lady. They traveled to their California ranch for longer vacations. Their general practice on the many weekends they spent at Camp David was to board the helicopter at the White House late Friday afternoon and return Sunday evening. (Courtesy Ronald Reagan Library.)

Reagan noted that the few oak trees on the White House grounds provided a meager supply of acorns for the many squirrels that made their home at the presidential estate. Consequently, he made it a practice to gather acorns at Camp David to provide sustenance for his furry friends. In this photograph, Reagan is returning to the White House from Camp David with a satchel of acorns. (Courtesy of Ronald Reagan Library.)

Mexico's president, Jose Lopez Portillo, was the first of three heads of state who visited President Reagan at Camp David during his two terms in office (above). Lopez Portillo and his wife were guests of the president and Nancy in June 1981. Like Reagan, the Mexican leader was an avid horseback rider. Indeed, prior to Reagan's inauguration in January 1981, Lopez Portillo had gifted him his personal mount, El Alamein. In addition to working sessions at the lodge, the two presidents conducted some of their business on horseback (right). In the evening, the Reagans hosted a large barbeque attended by Washington dignitaries, including several congressmen, cabinet members, and the chief justice of the Supreme Court. (Above, courtesy of Thurmont Main Street; right, courtesy of Ronald Reagan Library.)

After graduating from college in 1932, Reagan went to work for radio station WOC in Davenport, Iowa, as a sports announcer. He continued to use his broadcasting skills at various points in his career. Early in his presidency, he inaugurated a weekly radio talk on a variety of timely domestic and international topics. Prior to each five-minute broadcast, Reagan would take a swallow of hot water, a practice he reportedly learned from Frank Sinatra and a preacher. During his eight years in office, Reagan delivered over 150 radio addresses from Camp David. (Courtesy of Ronald Reagan Library.)

Nancy Reagan's signature focus as first lady was the war on drugs. Her "Just Say No" slogan became a popular nationwide mantra for the many people and organizations she enlisted in her cause. On October 2, 1982, she joined her husband in his weekly broadcast to address the issue of drug use and abuse. (Courtesy of Ronald Reagan Library.)

Judging from their careers as actors and public figures, one might expect that the president and first lady reveled in the attention focused on them. The first couple, however, strongly valued their personal time and viewed Camp David as a true retreat. They drew a clear line between the meetings and public events of the week and the quiet weekends at the camp. The president's staff were aware of this, and when possible, avoided intruding on the couple. The president and Nancy followed a simple routine that generally involved horseback riding, long walks, reading, and, at times, use of the camp's recreational facilities. Both regularly worked out at the camp's gym. Their meals generally simple. As at the White House, the president and his family were responsible for the cost of their meals. (Courtesy of Ronald Reagan Library.)

On April 13, 1986, President Reagan met with Japanese prime minister Yasuhiro Nakasone at Camp David. The discussions covered a wide range of topics, including Japanese support of US efforts to negotiate arms control agreements with the Soviet Union, and maintaining US–Japanese cooperation on defense issues. Most importantly, the two leaders discussed Japan's large trade surplus and the imbalance of imports and exports between the United States and Japan. Reagan and Nakasone agreed that the United States would take measures to increase exports, and Japan would work toward increasing imports. The talks went well, and the two heads of state spent an affable day at Camp David. (Both, courtesy of Ronald Reagan Library.)

During their 52 years of marriage, Ronald and Nancy Reagan were the closest of friends and mutual supporters. They met in 1949, shortly after Ronald's divorce from actress Jane Wyman, and after a three-year courtship, married in 1952. Nancy was in 11 movies before retiring from acting in 1959. The couple appeared together in one movie, *Hellcats in the Navy*, in 1957. As Ronald's career slowed and he made the transition to politics, Nancy was his chief supporter and advisor. The latter role raised some hackles, but as she wrote in her memoirs, "For eight years I was sleeping with the president, and if that doesn't give you special access, I don't know what does." The Reagans were not shy about showing their deep fondness for one another. At Camp David, the couple was generally able to escape the political world long enough to share special occasions. In the above photograph, they are celebrating Nancy's 64th birthday. Below, President Reagan is presenting a Valentine Day's gift to his first lady. (Both, courtesy of Ronald Reagan Library.)

Reagan once told an aide that "the best thing for the inside of a man is the outside of a horse." Nancy often rode with him as well as family members when they visited Camp David or the couple's Rancho del Cielo. In this photograph taken in the autumn of 1983, the president is joined on a horseback ride by Nancy, their son Ron, and Ron's wife, Doria. (Courtesy of Ronald Reagan Library.)

When President Reagan and the first lady rode together, their regimen included the president helping his wife dismount. A Reagan biographer noted that the couple was very firm in following this procedure. He relates that, on one occasion, a Secret Service agent moved toward the first lady to assist her and was intercepted by the president, who said, "That's *my* wife and *I'll* be the one to help her." (Courtesy of Ronald Reagan Library.)

The third and last head of state to visit Reagan at Camp David was Margaret Thatcher, prime minister of the United Kingdom. In December 1984, Thatcher was in Beijing and asked if she could meet with the president on her way home. Reagan planned to be at Camp David and invited her to join him for a luncheon meeting. The president, at the time, was promoting his administration's idea of developing a system to intercept ballistic missiles. His Strategic Defense Initiative, dubbed "Star Wars," was a controversial issue in the United States. Thatcher, a trained chemist, pointed out the difficulties in developing such a system. In the joint communique issued after the meeting, the two agreed that the United States and United Kingdom would negotiate before a system was deployed. Two years later, following summit talks between Reagan and Gorbachev, Thatcher met again at Camp David where the prime minister reportedly suggested that the president temper his arms reduction aims. (Both, courtesy of Ronald Reagan Library.)

Far and above any other activity, with the possible exception of horseback riding, the first couple enjoyed viewing movies at Camp David. As former actors and, in the president's case, a past president of the Screen Actors Guild, they knew the motion picture industry well. Mark Weinberg, a former press aide who traveled with the Reagans on most trips to Camp David, described the usual procedure on movie nights: "Without fail, at 7:45 the front door [of Aspen Lodge] would open and President Reagan would usher in guests, which usually included his personal aide, physician, military aide, senior Secret Service agent in charge, Marine One pilot, senior White House Communications officer and [Weinberg]." Rather than using a modern (for its time) VCR, the mini-theater was fitted with a projector showing actual reels. The Reagans viewed virtually every major motion picture of the 1980s but seemed to favor older films, including some that included the president or Nancy. At times, he enjoyed regaling his guests with amusing stories from his acting days. In all, the Reagans watched over 300 films during his tenure. (Courtesy of Ronald Reagan Library.)

Religious services at Camp David were generally held at Hickory Lodge. Presidents and their families occasionally traveled the short distance to Thurmont to attend Sunday services. In the early 1980s, Kenneth Plummer, a local contractor with long ties to Camp David, developed an idea for the construction of a permanent chapel at Camp David. The Reagans contributed $1,000 to the project, and on July 2, 1988, took part in the groundbreaking ceremony. (Courtesy of Ronald Reagan Library.)

Like many other first couples, the Reagans were doting "parents" of pets. In this 1988 photograph, the president and Nancy are taking a winter stroll at Camp David with their dog, Rex. Note the warm and stylish outfit that Rex is wearing. (Courtesy of Thurmont Main Street.)

Although some renovations had occurred under previous presidents, many of the cabins and facilities were showing their age. Over Nancy's years in public life, she had been criticized as an extravagant spender. During her husband's administration, she made modest interior changes to Aspen Lodge and several cabins and worked with the camp commander and outside consultants on structural changes such as enlargement of the main kitchen. She later wrote that "there was not a whisper of controversy . . . because the entire place is off limits to the press, nobody ever knew what I did." One alteration involved lowering the bottom of the windows in the Aspen Lodge so that the outside could be seen while seated. This can be seen in the above photograph of the Reagans greeting Prime Minister Thatcher in Aspen. The beautifully landscaped front of the lodge is shown in the photograph below. (Both, courtesy of Ronald Reagan Library.)

Eight

41

George H.W. Bush

Much like the Reagans, George and Barbara Bush thoroughly enjoyed Camp David and visited often. Also like the Reagans and other presidential couples, they owned a much-loved family homestead. The president and Barbara traditionally vacationed at their seaside home in Kennebunkport, Maine, and used Camp David as a getaway. In the four years of the Bush presidency, George and Barbara visited the retreat 124 times, averaging three weekends per month.

The Bushes welcomed guests and family to share the retreat with them and hosted a record number of foreign leaders. The atmosphere was strictly casual. President Bush had a firm rule about the dress code: No ties allowed.

The president and family members utilized virtually all of the recreational facilities at the camp. The president would sometimes leave the retreat to golf at nearby courses or to fish at a couple of favorite local ponds. He attended a minor-league baseball game in each of the two nearest cities, Frederick and Hagerstown.

The first couple was relaxed and considerate in their interactions with the camp's staff and were well-liked. The president and family members sometimes drew staff members into their sporting competitions.

President Bush and the first lady loved having their grandchildren visit the camp and had a playground constructed for them.

On New Year's Eve in 1990, in the midst of the Iraq war, the president wrote a touching letter to his five children. He expressed deep concern regarding the dangers facing US personnel and the sacrifices they were being called on to make. He was keenly aware of the impact his decisions as president made on the lives of the many people involved in the struggle. As a father, the president expressed his awareness of how blessed he and the family were and the joy he felt seeing them together. In closing, he told his children, "I am the luckiest Dad in the whole wide world."

Much like the Reagans, George and Barbara Bush thoroughly enjoyed Camp David and visited often. They also, like other presidential couples, owned a much-loved family homestead. The president and Barbara traditionally vacationed at their seaside home in Kennebunkport, using Camp David for shorter getaways. In the four years of the Bush presidency, George and Barbara visited the retreat 124 times. In the above picture, taken in September 1989, the Bushes are walking on the South Lawn of the White House toward Marine One for the brief flight to Camp David. Below, the president is sporting his personalized Camp David jacket while relaxing with Barbara. (Both, courtesy of the G.H.W. Bush Library.)

Camp David was a lively place when George and Barbara Bush were in residence. The president generally spent the early part of each day working in his office at Laurel Lodge but enthusiastically engaged in a wide variety of physical activities afterwards. Horseshoes was at the top of his list of favorites. Early in his administration, he had a horseshoe pit constructed at the camp and made frequent use of it. Guests, including heads of state, were not exempt from a presidential challenge. In the photograph above, Bush matches skills with Australian prime minister Robert Hawke. Below, he engages a member of the White House carpentry crew in a match. (Both, courtesy of G.H.W. Bush Library.)

In June 1990, Soviet leader Mikhail Gorbachev came to the United States to discuss European security issues. During a visit to Camp David, President Bush learned that his Soviet counterpart had never been introduced to the game of horseshoes. Bush instructed Gorbachev on the mechanics of the sport and invited him to try it (left). The Soviet leader threw a ringer on his first toss. That evening, Bush presented Gorbachev with a horseshoe mounted on a plaque (below). (Both, courtesy of G.H.W. Bush Library.)

Tennis was among the many sports the president enjoyed at Camp David. On occasion, he would supplement matches with family and guests by inviting someone with a bit more talent. Among the celebrities who visited the camp were tennis stars Andre Agassi and Chris Evert. The latter was his doubles partner in a match in August 1990. (Courtesy of G.H.W. Bush Library.)

The basement of Hickory Lodge houses a two-lane bowling alley constructed during the Eisenhower administration. In January 1993, Canadian prime minister Brian Mulroney visited the United States for talks, primarily related to trade. He and his family were guests of the Bushes at Camp David. In this photograph, the Mulroney children are trying out the lanes while Mila Mulroney and Barbara Bush watch in the background. (Courtesy of G.H.W. Bush Library.)

When snow fell at Camp David, it was time to drag out the toboggans. Dignity went by the wayside as the president, guests, and family hurtled down the hills. Bush loved frolicking with his grandchildren and seemed to enjoy snowy mishaps (above). When Arnold Schwarzenegger and his wife, Maria Shriver, were guests at Camp David, the "Terminator" joined the president for a downhill run, which apparently ended in a wipeout (left). Bush later sent this photograph to Schwarzenegger with the humorous inscription: "Turn, dammit, turn." In an unfortunate incident, Barbara Bush hit a tree while sledding and broke her leg. She was confined to a wheelchair for several days and hobbled around on crutches for several more. (Both, courtesy of G.H.W. Bush Library.)

The president was highly proficient at a sport called wallyball. The game is played over a net on a walled court and is often described as a hybrid of volleyball and racquetball or squash. Bush enjoyed drawing guests to the court for a bit of vigorous competition. In this photograph, national security advisor Brent Skowcroft is the president's doubles partner. (Courtesy of G.H.W. Bush Library.)

The area around Camp David contains several excellent fishing spots. FDR initiated the practice of leaving the bounds of the presidential retreat to try his luck at angling. Several of his successors followed suit, including Bush, who was an avid fisherman. While he favored sportfishing, the president enjoyed an occasional local outing during visits to Camp David. (Courtesy of National Park Service, Catoctin Mountain Park.)

President Bush was a great fan of Tex-Mex food. He particularly liked the fajitas and tamales prepared by family cook Paula Rondoon, who often traveled to Camp David with the Bushes. The fare was not always Tex-Mex, as can be seen in this photograph taken at Thanksgiving 1989 in the Aspen Lodge kitchen. (Courtesy of G.H.W. Bush Library.)

Country music was one of Bush's favorite genres. During his term in office, he hosted several country music artists at Camp David, including the Gatlin Brothers, Barbara Mandrell, and Lee Greenwood. In this photograph, George Strait is performing in the camp's chapel after dining with the Bushes and the family of Canadian prime minister Brian Mulroney. (Courtesy of G.W.H. Bush Library.)

On June 27, 1992, the president's daughter Dorothy "Doro" Bush-LeBlond and Robert Koch were married in the first-ever wedding at Camp David's Evergreen Chapel (right). Doro chose the presidential retreat as the venue for the wedding to avoid the tumult of a White House wedding. The Republican Bush family welcomed the groom into the fold even though he was a Democrat and chief of staff for a Democratic congressman! The president escorted his daughter down the aisle while music was played in the balcony (below). Afterwards, the wedding party and the 130 guests moved to the Aspen Lodge for the reception. (Both, courtesy of G.H.W. Library.)

During his four years in office, President Bush welcomed 18 foreign leaders to Camp David. The retreat provided a warm, relaxed environment for the leaders to get to know each other while addressing important matters of state. An invitation to Camp David was coveted in many international circles as a statement of stature and respect. Bush's guests included German chancellor Helmut Kohl, UK prime ministers Margaret Thatcher and John Major, Soviet president Mikhail Gorbachev and Russian president Boris Yeltsin, Mexican president Carlos Salinas de Gortari, and Japanese prime minister Kiichi Miyazawa. Aside from walking, the primary means of transportation on the grounds of the retreat was Golf Cart One. Like most of his predecessors, Bush enjoyed driving visitors on a tour of the camp's facilities and trails. In the photograph above, the president is preparing to take Margaret Thatcher for a spin. Below, Bush has found another horseshoes partner—Thatcher's successor as prime minister, John Major. (Both, courtesy of G.H.W. Bush Library.)

George and Barbara Bush had six children: four boys and two girls (daughter Robin died in infancy). Christmas was a special time for the far-flung family to come together. The Bush clan gathered at Camp David each Christmas during the four years of the G.H.W. Bush administration. Like their father, the Bush children were an active bunch and engaged in virtually all the activities available at the retreat. Meanwhile, Camp David offered infinite possibilities for the grandchildren to play and for their grandparents to dote on them. In the photograph above, 23 Bush family members are gathered at Camp David for the 1989 Christmas holidays. Below, the president has gathered seven grandchildren for a book reading session in Aspen Lodge. (Both, courtesy of G.H.W. Bush Library.)

There was no dedicated place of worship at Camp David for the first 40 years of its existence. Presidents could attend Sunday services at the Hickory Lodge, or they could travel to nearby Thurmont to worship at one of the town's churches. As noted in chapter seven, a plan for the construction of a chapel on the grounds of the retreat was developed during the Reagan years. The cost of the chapel's construction was about $1 million, all of which was raised from private, non-government sources. In 1991, President Bush presided over the dedication of Camp David's new Evergreen Chapel (above). (Both, courtesy of G.H.W. Bush Library.)

Nine

TURN OF THE CENTURY
BILL CLINTON AND GEORGE W. BUSH

Bill and Hillary Clinton's first visit to Camp David came a week after his inauguration in January 1993, when the president hosted a retreat for his cabinet members and senior staff. Some attendees were not enamored with the camp. George Stephanopoulos was reported to have likened the camp to a cheap mountain resort. Nevertheless, the president and first lady hosted several sessions during the weekend to discuss policy and set the tone for his administration.

Although Clinton initially seemed to view the camp primarily as a place to conduct meetings and other affairs of state, he and Hillary came to enjoy Camp David's "getaway" aspects. The family engaged in many of the recreational offerings, including biking, golfing, bowling, and cross-country skiing. They hosted a variety of guests, including heads of state, government officials, and celebrities. Their daughter, Chelsea, celebrated her 16th birthday at the camp with a party attended by school friends. Ultimately, during his eight years in office, President Clinton spent 173 days at the camp.

George W. Bush picked up where his father left off. In his biography of his father, George W. Bush recounts how the family gathered at Camp David in 1992, a month before his dad's administration came to an end, for what they believed would be their last Christmas at the retreat. Nine years later, they learned that they were wrong. The younger President Bush visited Camp David 149 times during his two terms in office.

The younger Bush was every much as active as his dad. He and his family—wife Laura and their twin daughters, Jenna and Barbara—were frequent and enthusiastic visitors to Camp David. While the new president continued the family tradition of utilizing virtually all of the camp's recreational facilities, he had his own favorites. George W. was an avid bicycler and frequently went on exhaustive rides with family and guests. During his tenure, a rock-climbing wall and batting cage were added to the camp's facilities.

George W.'s presidency was marked by the September 11, 2001, attacks on the US homeland. Camp David served as a safe zone on the day of the attacks and was used extensively in the following weeks for deliberations on the US response. The president also used the camp as a venue for hosting foreign heads of state. He welcomed 19 leaders to the camp during his tenure, including Russian president Vladimir Putin, British prime minister Tony Blair, and Egyptian president Hosni Mubarak.

Thanksgiving came to be a family tradition during President Clinton's two-term tenure. The president was a great lover of Southern-style fried cooking, but the family stuck to the traditional turkey and stuffing fare, with Bill doing the carving (above). The first Thanksgiving at Camp David was bittersweet. Bill's mother was able to join them but passed away the following year. (Courtesy of William J. Clinton Library.)

President Clinton enjoyed singing, and reportedly had an excellent voice. On Sundays when he was in residence at Camp David, he enthusiastically served as a member of the choir at services in the Evergreen Chapel. (Courtesy of William J. Clinton Library.)

Clinton enjoyed golf and frequently used the camp's driving range and a new fairway constructed near the Aspen Lodge. However, he found the three-hole course at Camp David not challenging enough. Instead, he played at several of the golf courses in the area. On these outings, in addition to the president's invited guests, security concerns dictated that he be accompanied by an entourage including his doctor, communications specialists, and, of course, Secret Service personnel. (Courtesy of William J. Clinton Library.)

Cross-country skiing offered an opportunity for Bill, Hillary, and Chelsea to share some family time. Chelsea often was accompanied to Camp David by a friend. Other winter activities included reading, games, and movies. The president would often do some television channel surfing at the camp. (Courtesy of William J. Clinton Library.)

In January 1998, the president hosted a screening of the movie *Good Will Hunting* at the Hickory Lodge's movie theater. The invitees included film actors, moviemakers, and some of the president's senior staff members (above). Among the Hollywood attendees were the stars of the movie, Matt Damon, Ben Affleck, Robin Williams, and Minnie Driver. In addition to the screening, the guests were treated to a five-course dinner at Laurel Lodge, a tour of Camp David, and use of some of the camp's facilities. The day after the screening, Clinton was joined by Damon and Affleck for an afternoon of watching football (below). (Both, courtesy of William J. Clinton Library.)

A major goal of the Clinton administration was finding a solution to the interminable struggle for peace in the Middle East. In 1993, after secret meetings in Oslo between representatives of Israel and the Palestinian people, delegations headed by Israeli prime minister Yitzhak Rabin and Palestinian leader Yasser Arafat came to Washington to sign a document aimed at promoting the peace process. Although the Clinton administration had not been involved in the Oslo negotiations, the president played a role in bringing the two sides together for the historic signing ceremony. Sadly however, in the ensuing years, problems and acrimony persisted. In the waning months of President Clinton's tenure, he persuaded Arafat and Israeli prime minister Ehud Barak to meet at Camp David in an attempt to settle major issues between the two sides. The talks lasted two weeks, but the leaders failed to reach an accord. In the above photograph, Barak, Clinton, and Arafat are strolling along one of the camp's many paths. Below, the three leaders continue the discussions. (Both, courtesy of William J. Clinton Library.)

Both President Clinton and the first lady enjoyed bowling and it was generally agreed—and often proven—that Hillary was the better bowler. Yet it was Bill who was the teacher when he heard that Secretary of State Madeleine Albright had never played. (Courtesy of William J. Clinton Library.)

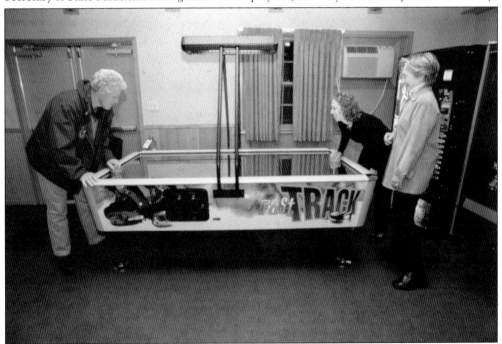

Indoor activities at the camp included an arcade of electronic games. In this photograph, Bill and Chelsea are battling in a game of Fast Track while Hillary observes the action. (Courtesy of William J. Clinton Library.)

George W. Bush continued the Christmas at Camp David tradition started by his father. In the years between the two Bush administrations, marriages and births significantly expanded the family. In this photograph taken at the camp during the 2008 Christmas holidays, 31 Bush family members are assembled for a group shot. At their Christmas Eve dinner, the family feasted on Tex-Mex food: enchiladas, tamales, guacamole, rice, and beans. Christmas Day lunch featured traditional turkey with dressing. (Courtesy of George W. Bush Library.)

During the Christmas 2008 family gathering, the large Bush clan made ample use of the retreat's facilities, engaging in boisterous family competitions at the wallyball courts and, as seen in this photograph, the bowling alley. (Courtesy of George W. Bush Library.)

The Evergreen Chapel, formally dedicated by George H.W. Bush, was designed to welcome worshipers of all faiths. The sanctuary is devoid of religious symbols. Bush family members regularly attended services at the chapel. In this photograph, the 41st and 43rd presidents and their families are singing hymns at a Sunday service. (Courtesy of George W. Bush Library.)

Much like his father, George W. seemed always on the move at Camp David. He was an avid jogger and was not shy about inviting guests and camp personnel to join him on his daily run or on power walks. Here, he is accompanied by First Lady Laura Bush, brother Marvin Bush, White House chief of staff Andy Card, and Card's wife, Kathleene, on a brisk ramble around the camp. (Courtesy of George W. Bush Library.)

Bicycling was among George W.'s favorite activities at the retreat, and as with other activities, he attacked it vigorously. Former camp commander Michael Giorgione cites an occasion on which the pilot of Marine One was invited to accompany the president and guests on a ride. He showed up with a cheap loner bike and later observed that "it was a bit like showing up to a Ferrari convention in a Volkswagen bus." In this photograph, the president is accompanied by Danish prime minister Anders Fogh Rasmussen. (Courtesy of George W. Bush Library.)

On September 11, 2001, President Bush was in Florida reading to children at an elementary school when terrorists struck the World Trade Center and the Pentagon. The Secret Service moved Vice President Cheney to the White House's command center bunker while the president flew back to Washington. To ensure continuity of power, Cheney and his wife were flown that evening to the relative safety of Camp David (above). The following day, President Bush joined him and members of the national security staff to begin planning a course of action (below). US intelligence quickly identified the attackers as members of the terrorist Al Qaeda organization, based in the mountains of Afghanistan and harbored by the Taliban government. In the ensuing weeks, the United States and its allies launched a military incursion into Afghanistan and deposed the Taliban rulers. (Both, courtesy of National Archives.)

In the aftermath of the 1991 Iraq War, Pres. George H.W. Bush was criticized for not sending troops to Baghdad to remove Iraqi dictator Saddam Hussein from power. Iraqi actions in the ensuing years led to the Gulf War of 2003. Camp David again was the scene of top-level meetings to plan and execute a military operation aimed at vanquishing the country's military forces and deposing Hussein. In the photograph above, President Bush is flanked by Vice Pres. Dick Cheney and Secretary of State Condoleezza Rice during discussions at Camp David about the Gulf War. (Courtesy of Thurmont Main Street.)

Camp David has a long history of visits by presidential pets, beginning with FDR's famous dog, Fala. The senior President Bush's dogs, Millie and her son Ranger, often accompanied their parents to the camp. A decade later, a George W. Bush family pet, Barney, seemed to feel entitled to the grand entrance accorded visiting dignitaries. The president enjoyed his company, noting that Barney "never discussed politics and was always a faithful friend." (Courtesy of George W. Bush Library.)

During his eight years in office, George W. hosted 19 foreign leaders at Camp David, more than any other president. Among the heads of state invited to the retreat were Russian president Vladimir Putin, British prime minister Tony Blair, Japanese prime minister Junichiro Koizumi, and Egyptian president Hosni Mubarak. Bush sought to create a relaxed and friendly atmosphere at the retreat, encouraging guests to join him in some of the varied activities available. In the photograph above, the president—a one-time managing general partner of baseball's Texas Rangers—is playing catch with Prime Minister Koizumi. Below, Bush is giving Danish prime minister Anders Fogh Rasmussen a ride in Golf Cart One. (Both, courtesy of Thurmont Main Street.)

In the two years prior to Russian president Vladimir Putin's visit to Camp David in 2003, the United States withdrew from the 1972 Anti-Ballistic Missile Treaty and signed a treaty aimed at reducing each country's arsenal of nuclear weapons. At the Camp David talks in September 2003, the two sides confirmed a commitment to cooperate on a variety of matters. (Courtesy of George W. Bush Library.)

In June 2002, Egyptian president Hosni Mubarak met with President Bush at Camp David. The primary discussion centered on the continued vexing problems in the Middle East, particularly relations between the Israelis and Palestinians. (Courtesy of George W. Bush Library.)

In July 2001, President Bush traveled to New York's Ellis Island to attend a swearing-in ceremony for new US citizens. Guests included New York officials with the governor and representatives from Bush's administration. The president pointed out that two of the guests from his administration came to the United States as immigrants. Elaine Chou (secretary of labor) and Mel Martinez (secretary of housing and urban development) "are Americans by choice," Bush stated. During the president's term of office, each were guests at Camp David. For Chou, the visit was her second to the retreat. In 1992, she and her husband, Sen. Mitch McConnell, were hosted by President Bush's father, George H.W. Bush. Martinez visited the camp in October 2001. In the photograph above, President Bush and Martinez are at the Camp David golf course. The president is the pitcher, and Martinez is the catcher. Below, Elaine Chou, Mitch McConnell, President Bush, Laura Bush, and others watch a movie at Hickory Lodge. (Both, courtesy of George W. Bush Library.)

Ten

CHANGES OF COMMAND

BARACK OBAMA, DONALD TRUMP, AND JOE BIDEN

When Pres. Barack Obama took office in 2008, he was not expected to make extensive use of Camp David. First Lady Michelle Obama noted that "he's an urban guy." He was also the father of two young girls who would be involved in an array of school and social activities in Washington. The president and Michelle wanted their daughters to have as normal a life as possible and were reluctant to pull them from weekend activities in their new Washington home. The family spent vacation time in the president's original home state of Hawaii or at properties of friends and backers in Martha's Vineyard, Massachusetts. Consequently, during his eight years in office, the president visited Camp David only 39 times.

Among President Obama's favored activities at Camp David were basketball, skeet shooting, and workouts in the retreat's gym. Michelle occasionally hosted friends at the camp. Family visits were relaxed and informal, with easy interaction with camp personnel and their families.

In May 2012, Chicago was slated to be the site of the G8 Summit, an annual gathering that brought together the heads of eight leading industrial nations. In the face of potentially large, disruptive protests, the location of the summit was changed to Camp David. The new venue proved conducive to a relaxed atmosphere and constructive meetings.

Pres. Donald Trump made his first visit to Camp David on Father's Day 2017, becoming the 14th president to utilize the retreat. He was accompanied by First Lady Melania Trump, the couple's son Barron, and Melania's parents. In the early days of his administration, Trump indicated that he would not be spending much time at the retreat. However, in remarks after this inaugural visit, he referred to the camp as "beautiful" and "a very special place." During his four years in office, President Trump visited Camp David 15 times.

When Pres. Joe Biden took office in January 2021, he already was a veteran visitor to Camp David, having spent time there during his eight years as vice president in the Obama administration. Echoing Ronald Reagan, he noted that living in the White House is "a little like a gilded cage in terms of being able to walk outside and do things." He spends his getaway time at his home in Wilmington, Delaware; a summer house in Rehoboth Beach, Delaware; and Camp David.

In 1975, leaders of six advanced industrialized nations met to discuss economic and political concerns and try to reach mutual understandings on these and other international issues. The group expanded to eight countries in 1998: the United States, France, Italy, Japan, the United Kingdom, West Germany, Canada, and Russia. In 2012, the United States hosted the annual meeting. It was originally scheduled to be held in Chicago, but the prospect of protests by groups opposed to globalization led to a change of venue to the relative seclusion of Camp David. The G8 met for two days, and at the conclusion of the conference, issued a 40-point declaration outlining understandings (but not always agreement) on a variety of international issues. In the photograph above, the attendees are gathered for a working dinner. Clockwise from President Obama are Prime Minister David Cameron (United Kingdom), Prime Minister Dmitry Medvedev (Russia), Chancellor Angela Merkel (Germany), Pres. Herman Van Rompuy (European Council), Pres. Jose Manuel Barroso (European Commission), Prime Minister Yoshihiko Noda (Japan), Prime Minister Mario Monti (Italy), Prime Minister Stephen Harper (Canada), and Pres. Francois Hollande (France). Below, the group has convened for discussions on the patio of Laurel Lodge. (Both, courtesy of White House.)

President Obama believed that a relaxed, relatively informal atmosphere would be most conducive to meaningful talks. There was no dress code, and participants were encouraged to enjoy the trails and other amenities. Here, several leaders have settled in the living room of Aspen Lodge to continue their conversations. Clockwise from Obama are President Hollande, Prime Minister Monti, and Chancellor Merkel. (Courtesy of White House.)

The G8 Summit coincided with the Champions League soccer final between Bayern Munich and Chelsea. The match ended in a tie decided by a shootout. Chelsea won 4-3. This was a "don't miss" match, and a large group of leaders and staff gathered to watch and cheer. (Courtesy of White House.)

The kitchen staff at Camp David had to be prepared for many types of culinary contingencies. At the G8 Summit, Prime Minister Noda was two days away from his 55th birthday, so the staff prepared a chocolate cake for the occasion. Seated with the prime minister are, from left to right, President Barroso, Prime Minister Monti, and Prime Minister Harper. (Courtesy of White House.)

During President Obama's first term in office, Wendy Halsey became Camp David's first female commander. She came aboard in June 2011, accompanied by her husband and three children. In his memoir of his days at Camp David, former camp commander Michael Giorgione notes that Halsey's service during the G8 Summit was a highlight of her tour. In this photograph, she is sharing a light moment with Obama and Command Master Al Marcucci shortly after the president's arrival. (Courtesy of White House.)

In the 1950s, President Eisenhower had the Brunswick Corporation set up four billiard tables at Camp David. The company reports that Presidents Kennedy, Nixon, Carter, and Clinton made use of the tables. Here, President Obama is winding down after the conclusion of the G8 Summit. (Courtesy of White House.)

A year after the G8, President Obama hosted a meeting of the Gulf Cooperation Council (GCC) at Camp David. The GCC is comprised of six Gulf countries and was organized in 1981 to foster cooperation on economic, social, and political matters affecting its members. In May 2015, Obama invited the GCC leaders to Camp David to discuss strengthening cooperation between member nations and the United States. Here, Obama is shaking hands with Sheikh Sabah Al-Ahmad Al-Jabar Al Sabah, amir of Kuwait. (Courtesy White House.)

In March 2015, Camp David served as a venue for a day of high-level meetings between officials from the United States and Afghanistan. The US delegation was headed by Secretary of State John Kerry and included Secretary of the Treasury Jacob Lew and Secretary of Defense Ash Carter. The Afghan contingent was led by Pres. Ashraf Ghani. The discussions focused on US-Afghan security and economic development issues. (Courtesy of White House.)

US presidents are never off duty. Camp David is fitted with the technology and staffing needed for a president to be in constant contact and command. On August 6, 2011, US Navy SEAL Team Six—the unit that had killed Osama Bin Laden—experienced the costliest day in its storied history. A helicopter carrying 30 US troops, including 17 from SEAL Team Six, was shot down during an operation against a Taliban compound. President Obama was at Camp David and, in this photograph, is on the phone being briefed on the situation. (Courtesy of White House.)

Sasha Obama celebrated her 10th birthday with a pool party at Camp David. The first father seems to be having an excellent time harassing his daughter with a water pistol. (Courtesy of White House.)

Basketball was one of Obama's passions. He shot hoops many times and in many places during his presidency. Here, he has engaged senior staff members and some of their families in a pickup game at the Leatherwood Court in Camp David's Wye Oak athletic center. (Courtesy of White House.)

In August 2017, President Trump convened a weekend of meetings with his cabinet at Camp David to discuss the situation in Afghanistan. Major issues discussed were the status of the war, the level of US troop strength, and strategy regarding Pakistan. Vice President Mike Pence was traveling in Latin America but cut his trip short to attend the meetings (above). Over the weekend, the president signed a bill authorizing the establishment of a Global War on Terrorism Memorial. He also signed into law three bills related to domestic issues. In the photograph below, the president is surrounded by members of his national security team. (Both, courtesy of White House.)

Trump was sometimes joined by other family members on visits to Camp David, but little is known about the activities of the president and his family during his non-business stays. In the above photograph, taken in December 2020, Trump is returning to the White House after a weekend at Camp David with grandchildren Arabella, Theodore, and Joseph Kushner. (Courtesy of White House.)

In September 2017, President Trump convened his cabinet at Camp David for a weekend discussion of a wide range of issues, including measures to pass a tax reform bill in Congress and the increasingly belligerent actions of North Korea's leader, Kim Jon Un. During the weekend, it became clear that the devastation of Hurricane Harvey two weeks earlier in Texas and Louisiana could be matched in Florida by the approaching Hurricane Irma. Here, the cabinet is meeting in the Laurel Lodge's conference room. (Courtesy of White House.)

On several occasions during his administration, Trump used Camp David as a venue for formally signing legislation into law. In September 2017, the president signed a bill at Camp David to provide disaster aid to areas affected by Hurricane Harvey as well as a controversial bill extending the US borrowing limit. (Courtesy of White House.)

In January 2018, the president was seeking congressional approval of several upcoming legislative measures and invited Republican leaders to join him for discussions at Camp David. The session was followed with a dinner that evening. In this photograph, the president is engaged in conversation with Senate Majority Leader Mitch McConnell. (Courtesy of White House.)

In the last days of August 2019, a devastating storm wreaked havoc on the Bahamas and headed toward the East Coast of the United States. The National Weather Service deemed Hurricane Dorian the strongest and most destructive of the 2019 hurricane season. President Trump was at Camp David during the final weekend of August and requested that the Federal Emergency Management Agency brief him on the hurricane's track. He was joined by Florida senator Rick Scott (above) and senior White House staff (below). At the time, the hurricane's path appeared to threaten the coasts of Florida, Georgia, South Carolina, and North Carolina. The president believed that the storm might hit Alabama, causing a controversy that lingered for months. The storm arrived on the US coast on September 5, and while it did significant damage in several areas, it had weakened and did not reach its feared level of destruction. (Both, courtesy of White House.)

As noted earlier, Joe Biden was not a stranger to Camp David when he became president. He had spent time at the retreat during his days as vice president in Barack Obama's administration, as seen here with the president and vice president relaxing at the camp's tennis courts during one of Biden's visits. The young girl is Claire Duncan, daughter of Obama's education secretary, Arne Duncan. (Courtesy of White House.)

President Biden reportedly spends several weeks working on major speeches and continues to make changes up to the last minute. He works closely with staff as a speech is drafted and rehearses before a podium to hone his delivery. In the photograph above, Biden and advisors are working on the 2023 State of the Union address. Seated at the table are, clockwise from lower left, deputy chief of staff Bruce Reed, senior advisor Mike Donilon, director of speechwriting Vinay Reddy, Biden, and counselor Steve Ricchetti. Below, the president is at the podium rehearsing the State of the Union address as staffers work in the foreground. (Both, courtesy of White House.)

Camp David is equipped to provide the president with the means to carry out most executive functions and stay abreast of late-breaking developments. In this photograph, taken in January 2022, the president is considering the situation leading up to the Russian invasion of Ukraine while following developments on multiple video monitors. (Courtesy of White House.)

While formal signing of legislative bills generally takes place at the White House or at a relevant location, it can also be done at Camp David. In March 2022, Congress passed a large and contentious bill needed to avoid a government shutdown. With an immediate deadline looming, it was necessary to pass a stopgap measure to allow time to prepare the bill for its formal enactment. The president was at Camp David and signed the extension there. (Courtesy of White House.)

Marine One is not your everyday helicopter. In fact, there are several Marine One helicopters. The term is actually the call sign for any helicopter transporting the president. The fleet of potential Marine Ones has varied over the years. Current models are large, comfortable aircraft. The usual route to Camp David begins on the South Lawn of the White House. On occasion, as in the above photograph of the helicopter taking President Biden to Camp David, Marine One will use Joint Base Andrews near Washington, DC. In the photograph below, President Biden and First Lady Jill Biden have just taken off from the South Lawn and are flying over the National Mall en route to Camp David. (Both, courtesy of White House.)

DISCOVER THOUSANDS OF LOCAL HISTORY BOOKS FEATURING MILLIONS OF VINTAGE IMAGES

Arcadia Publishing, the leading local history publisher in the United States, is committed to making history accessible and meaningful through publishing books that celebrate and preserve the heritage of America's people and places.

Find more books like this at
www.arcadiapublishing.com

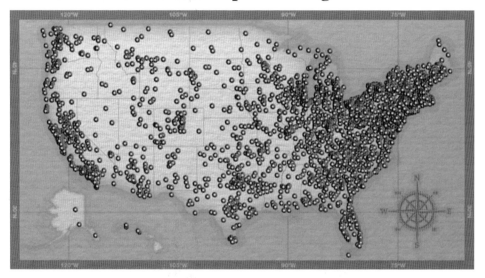

Search for your hometown history, your old stomping grounds, and even your favorite sports team.